MW01278148

**REDEFINING THE VALUE OF VALUES TO
DRIVE BUSINESS RESULTS**

VALUES
CULTURE
PERIOD

COREY ATKINSON, AYO OWODUNNI

Values. Culture. Period.
Redefining the value of values to drive business results
Corey Atkinson & Ayo Owodunni

Values. Culture. Period.
Copyright © 2021 by Corey Atkinson & Ayo Owodunni

Editors: Carolyn R. Wilker & Ace Writers Ventures
Cover design: Farrukh Khan

Publication Data
Atkinson, Corey & Owodunni, Ayo
Values. Culture. Period. - Redefining the value of values to drive business results
Hardcover ISBN: 978-1-7779381-2-3
Paperback ISBN: 978-1-7779381-0-9
eBook ISBN: 978-1-7779381-1-6

For information about this book, please contact:
www.valuescultureperiod.com
info@valuescultureperiod.com

Praise For

VALUES.CULTURE.PERIOD.

"Reality on paper...learning how to approach developing organizational culture in a practical way. Atkinson and Owodunni have put together a great read that clearly breakdowns culture and a practice model to get it right."

- **Jasmine Antonio**, VP, HR Global, Caesarstone

"The authors' storytelling approach in *Values. Culture. Period.* will energize leaders across all industries to do the important work of identifying their organizations' values and then reap the rewards of an improved culture, employee engagement and productivity."

- **Paul A. Mitcham**, City of Mississauga City Manager and Chief Administrative Officer

"In this impressive debut, Atkinson & Owodunni weave two engaging stories of change, emotion and trust all building to the power intentional leadership. Like its very different protagonists—Guy and Katherine—*Values. Culture. Period.* brings value from beginning to end."

- **Dr. Rouba Fattal**, Sr. Policy Advisor – Innovation, Science & Economic Development, Canada

"Helpful supplemental material for students and entrepreneurs which illustrates, through an engaging fictional narrative, the authors' positive insights on improving corporate cultures."

- **Boris Tsimerinov**, CEO, Semper8

"Looking to transform your corporate culture? Then read this book!"

- **Andrew Nevin**, Partner, PwC West Africa

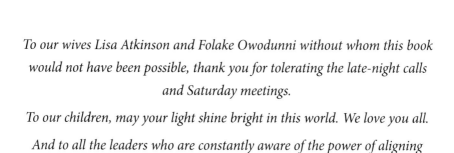

To our wives Lisa Atkinson and Folake Owodunni without whom this book would not have been possible, thank you for tolerating the late-night calls and Saturday meetings.

To our children, may your light shine bright in this world. We love you all.

And to all the leaders who are constantly aware of the power of aligning values to bring about positive change. Continue to be a model of consistency for those around you.

FOREWORD

VALUES AND CULTURE are topics that impact every part of our lives—business, diversity, relationships, opportunities—the list goes on. But given their presence in all that we do, we do not give them the required conversations and focus needed for balance and success.

Values create friendships and movements, but they also interfere with understanding and minimize growth. To dramatically improve our work and personal worlds, in Values Culture Period we focus on two perspectives:

1. the challenges that come with sidestepping a value conversation in organizations; and

2. the opportunities that arise when organizations truly embody the core values and the impact they have on a desired organizational culture.

As you read this book, keep in mind what values are and what they are not. Integrity, profitability, growth, resilience, and exceeding customer expectations are not examples of values, but are really just corporate strategies being positioned as values.

In *Values Culture Period*, we define values as concepts or ideas that clearly guide organizational thinking, actions, and desired results. Essentially, values are the behaviours that allow for the previously mentioned corporate strategies. When it comes to values and culture, actions speak louder than words.

As you read, you will learn about the critical steps organizations must take to create a culture where team members effectively operate to lead change and drive business results. But for values to be crystal clear, and culture to grow, organizations need to focus on the following habits: ongoing conversations, deep understanding of all performers, and strategic initiatives. It is our belief that these habits are the cornerstones of all culture—across all domains, situations, and histories. As our times become more pressing, our to-dos become longer and our relationships more frayed, then culture becomes more critical to our very existence.

This is nothing new for many of you reading this though. For decades, C-suite executives all the way to front-line employees have recognized that company culture contributes to profitability. But recognizing this *and making it work* has been a challenge. Until now.

In putting this book together, we have spent countless hours interviewing, studying, discussing, and absorbing the topic of values, culture, and employee engagement. This book will give you a deeper understanding of how values can help us, and hinder us, in driving change and leading a project team, or even considering a merger. Through the lens of two fictional companies, you will learn about value alignment, value sabotage, and the required everyday conversations that shapes a culture. By looking at the challenges of 1990 Tylenol, examples of leaders we have coached, and other examples from yesterday and today, readers will get a strategic look at how values can be sabotaged—even by the leader of an organization.

By following the framework of the *operationalizing values model* (OVM), you will have a step-by-step process to ensure that the critical areas—value definition and culture shaping—happen intentionally and with as few bumps as possible.

In the second half of the book, we will look at how to bring values to life and the type of leadership conversations and teamwork required to implement the *OVM*. The focus here is to show the critical conversations and steps that leaders, teams, and organizations must take to develop the values and culture.

Values. Culture. Period was written with a specific audience in mind.

Leaders in organizations large and small, and across all industries, looking to increase performance and make it sustainable.

Leaders curious about new ideas to engage and motivate their entire team roster.

Leaders in organizations committed to action, leading with intention, and supporting change.

Leaders at all levels of the organization interested and aware of the value of authentic communication and conversations.

Leaders looking for an insightful and proven method of leading a culture transformation regardless of industry, sector, or business environment.

Table of Contents

CHAPTER 1:

The Signing

"Without ethical culture, there is no salvation for humanity"
- Albert Einstein

IT'S ONLY 11:00 a.m. but Guy feels he's been putting out fires all morning at the office. He arrived around 7:30 a.m.; since then, he already had a stressful conversation with Desean, one of his western area managers, to discuss reports about a kitchen manager in a yelling match with one of their team members. From there he jumped into an emergency meeting with the Chief Financial Officer to discuss discrepancies in the revenue document meant to be shown to the board by the end of the week; and now he is in a meeting with corporate sales, listening to their multiple excuses—oops, reasons—on why business development was slow this quarter.

As Guy walked back to his office and past Sara, his executive assistant, he said, "Please hold off any other meetings for the next hour."

"Sure. I'll take care of that for you," Sara said, a bit concerned about the postponement. She quickly picked up the phone to reschedule his 11:00 a.m. and noon meetings.

Guy shut his door and slumped into his chair. All I seem to be doing here is constantly putting out fires. There has got to be a better way.

He looked out the window of his 15th floor office building to take in the skyline. It was beautiful this time of year. There were only a few trees in the downtown core, but the movement of the cars speeding out of and into the city gave him a sense of tranquility.

When he first started with the Toronto-based company, they were in the west end of the city in a three-story building. But as the organization grew in market share and profits, they were able to move to their current uptown location. He could now stare out into the horizon, gazing, thinking, and strategizing. Since becoming the President of Savos, a restaurant chain with 80 locations and 2,000 employees across the country, getting five minutes to himself to simply gaze at the city skyline was more of a mini escape to ground himself for the next wave of unpredictable challenges. A knock on his door robbed him of his tranquility.

It was Janni, the Vice President of HR. Guy looked out for Sara to figure out why she didn't stop Janni from walking in. From the look on Janni's face, there seemed to be a problem that needed to be addressed immediately. It was that type of day.

"What is it, Janni?" Guy sounded enthusiastic but nervous, hoping to get back to his moment of serenity.

"I think we might have a problem," she said.

"Well, what is it?" Guy said, trying to read the expression on her face as she sat down.

This was very unlike Janni. She usually handled these matters by herself. Guy was not sure why this one was different.

"Just got a call from one of our area managers out east. A new staff member who just started working recently approached her to ask a question about signing a union card. Turns out that the new employee was approached by another staff member to sign up."

"What? A union card? Which restaurant was that? Can we call to find out more to…?"

Janni cut Guy off immediately. "We cannot do that, Guy. We have to be very cautious. You know that labour laws have really strict rules on management behaviour during a union organizing drive."

"What do you mean management behaviour? How are we so sure that's what is happening? Shouldn't we try to figure out what the heck is going on?"

"Once we are aware of anything like this," Janni said, "we cannot be seen as campaigning against or interfering with the right to unionize."

"So, we just sit around and wait for them to represent our employees? I mean, how will this affect the business?" Guy quickly caught himself as Janni gave him a sign to stay calm.

"Well, our job right now is to sit and wait."

A call came through the office line, it was Sara.

"Guy, you have a call from one of the Board of Directors. It sounds like Ms. Peterson. She's on line 2."

"Thanks."

Guy looked at Janni while he reached for the phone pad to press line 2. "Sorry, this might take some time."

"No worries, Guy. I will call you when I get more information." She headed out of the office.

In the three years he'd been president of Savos, Guy recalled the company's pride in its chain of casual dining restaurants across Canada. Savos represented a memorable dining experience with fantastic food selection, welcoming spaces, and modern interiors. As a result, Savos has enjoyed great customer service ratings over the past ten years, consistently scoring over 4.5 stars across the country. Unfortunately, the customer was very different from the employee experience.

Since Guy joined the organization, turnover had always been a problem. However, due to the non-stop pace of the industry, nobody, including himself, had really paid much attention. As many say in the restaurant business, this is the nature of the beast. With some luck, though, Savos always found a way to hire new staff members, bring them up to speed, and get them in front of customers as quickly as possible. Sometimes success had a way of blinding you to your flaws. At least, that is how Guy had reasoned it so far. As Guy chatted with the board member, he couldn't help but think about what was happening at the restaurant and the employees who were looking to bring in a union.

Why would staff want a union? I thought we had created the environment and offered the flexibility for people to feel good about working here. What have I missed?

"Hey, Guy, are you there?" Ann Peterson's voice from the other end of the phone line jolted him back into reality.

"Sorry, Ann, yes, I can join the committee for a quick meeting tomorrow evening."

"Great. I will email you the agenda and start time later today. Bye." And with that Ann hung up.

Guy got off the call and stood staring out of his office window again. He needed to think and plan the next steps to take the organization out of the current situation.

While staring into the abyss, his office phone rang. It was Sara.

"You have a 4:15 p.m. meeting with Chief Information Officer Misha today. He has some updates for you on the new inventory software that is to be installed at the restaurants. The meeting should only last 20 minutes. But please remember that your son has a basketball game at 6:00 p.m. He is playing in Kitchener, so you'll need to leave right after to get there on time."

"And Janni just called to let you know that the Assistant Store Manager at the Vancouver North restaurant has handed in his two weeks' notice today. She said that you should be aware that this is the fourth notice from restaurant management in the past month."

"What!" Guy yelled with his inside voice. He was glad that Sara was not standing in front of him to see his reaction to this news. The fourth this month? What was going on? This was not good and he needed to get to the bottom of this quickly.

After a moment, he said, "Thank you, Sara. Please book a call with him for tomorrow. I'd like to personally wish him good luck."

"Okay, I'll do that."

As Guy moved from the window and slumped into his chair, there was a knock at the door. It was his 4:15 p.m. meeting with the CIO.

"Come in," he said, summoning the strength to keep the day going.

AWARD

"This year's Board of Trade Business Impact Award goes to TBO Bank's Director of Operations, Kathleen Brown!"

The room filled with applause once Kathleen's name was announced. The ballroom was filled with about 100 professionals from across the Toronto area. Kathleen walked up to the podium to accept her award and give her speech.

She had never been good at standing in front of a crowd to make a speech. Despite being a strong and resourceful leader at TBO, Kathleen always tried to shy away from the spotlight. Thank heavens for presentation coaches! The last time she had to give an acceptance speech was over 20 years ago at university. She smiled to herself as she remembered looking at out at her fellow students, opening her mouth—and nothing coming out.

This time Kathleen was ready. She stood at the podium, looked down at her notes and then looked at the audience, smiled, and said, "Thank you. Thank you all very much. I want to first thank the organizers of this event for honouring me. I'm very grateful. I would also like to thank my mentor, Bill Weathers, for really pushing me to become the leader I am today."

Many business leaders in the crowd knew and respected Bill. Kathleen could see heads nodding in the crowd.

"When I graduated from university, I thought I wanted to work in corporate finance. But, after six long months, I knew that finance was the biggest mistake of my life. After my second week in the role and trying to learn every formula Microsoft Excel had—I realized this was not for me. No offense to the amazing people who work in finance."

The crowd chuckled.

"Somehow I managed to reset and figure out what I really wanted to do. Where could I have an impact and make a difference? I ventured into sales and account management and quickly worked my way up in the Client Relationship & Experience Department. And then I met Bill Weathers on a train to Montreal a few years ago and that meeting created new opportunities for me. A quick pleasantry turned into a three-hour conversation about passions, teamwork, and making a mark. I don't know what Bill saw in a confused, young, and hungry single mother who was trying to balance family and career…but I am glad he looked beyond the confusion and invited me to join the TBO team."

The crowd started to clap again.

"In conclusion, I would like to encourage all of you—new or seasoned leaders—here today, take care of your people, and they will take care of your business. They do not care what you know…until they know that you care. Thank you, Bill. And thanks to all of you."

Kathleen walked off the stage, humble but proud of this accomplishment. She had come a long way in her career to achieve this Business Impact award.

During the networking session of the award ceremony, Kathleen approached the Board of Trade President and thanked her for a great event.

"Great job this year, Marissa. You and the team seem to keep setting the bar higher and higher."

"Thanks, and congratulations to you, Kat. You deserved that award. The team at TBO are lucky to have you."

A gentleman walked up to Marissa, waiting his turn for a quick conversation.

"Oh, perfect timing. Kathleen, please meet Guy. Guy, this is Kathleen. Guy is the President at Savos Restaurant and one of our newest members at the Board of Trade. He's been such a great asset to the board, and we truly value his expertise."

"A pleasure to meet you, Kathleen," Guy said with a slight Quebecois accent. "Congratulations! I'm sure you've heard that a few times today."

"A pleasure meeting you too," Kathleen replied to Guy. "Thank you. I truly feel honoured. I would love to stay and chat, but I have to head out. I have an urgent meeting. Looking forward to another get together soon, Marissa."

Kathleen left the event for her 2:00 p.m. meeting at the office. Her company was interviewing a few consultants, with the goal of selecting one of them to help implement new processes in the Retail Banking division. A big initiative that required her full attention.

Once Kathleen arrived at the office, she headed straight for the bank's meeting room floor. As she headed towards the boardroom, Bill, the CEO, stepped out of the elevator.

"Hey, Bill."

"Hey! How was the award ceremony?"

"It was great. I'm sure you knew I won. You could have given me a hint."

Bill gave his usual hearty laugh.

"Ah, you deserved it. I did not want to ruin the surprise. Congratulations!"

"Thank you, Bill. Sorry, I must run. I have a meeting with some consultants in exactly three minutes."

"Okay, I need to see you later. It's important."

His tone slightly changed as he shared this news with Kathleen. There was something that caught Kathleen's attention.

"Okay, Bill, see you after the meeting then."

After the meeting, Kathleen headed to Bill's office to find out about the important news. She was very curious about what he wanted to share. Was there an issue with the revamp proposal? she wondered.

She walked into Bill's office and found Marvin in there with him.

"Ah, you're just in time. Come on in." Bill waved her into the room.

As the Chief Marketing Officer at TBO Bank, Marvin was a candid communicator and a loyalist—as Kathleen liked to think of him—who had worked at TBO for almost 20 years. Marvin had been involved in wealth management, operations, and led the marketing team for the past four years.

"Hi, Marvin, how are you? Bill, what did you want to talk about?"

Marvin smiled and said hello to Kathleen.

"I'm glad both of you are here. I have an announcement to make, and I wanted both of you to hear it first."

"Bill, if this has to do with the structural revamps, give me another chance to rework the proposal with my team," Kathleen interrupted. "I can have it resent to you in three days. It is urgent that we push through with these major…"

"That's not it, Kathleen," Bill cut her off politely.

Kathleen stopped dead in her tracks in confusion. She looked at Marvin, who looked away from her once their eyes met.

"What is it, Bill?"

"Well, I'm retiring."

FIX

Guy finally had time to call Janni to finish their conversation from earlier in the day. He was on his drive to Kitchener.

"Hey, Janni, sorry we couldn't finish up earlier. Is this a good time?"

"Yes."

"I have been thinking and reflecting about our conversation earlier. Quite honestly, I have known things were challenging for some of our locations, but I never got the impression that they were this bad. It's just always been this way. I apologize for not discussing this with you before now."

"Well, turnover in our industry is usually quite high, Guy."

"You are right about that, but it shouldn't be a reason for us to lower the employee experience." Guy felt it was time they, rather he, stopped giving excuses. "Let's be honest with ourselves, Janni. I could have done better."

Both were silent on the phone. To Guy, it felt like they were finally realizing the truth—he had dropped the ball.

"Okay, so how about this?" Janni jumped in. "I have been doing some thinking as well and I think we can get ahead of this thing."

"What do you mean?"

"We don't know how long it will take to get 40 per cent to sign a union card."

"Okay."

"Even after signing, the application has to go to the Labour Board for final approval before we are served a notice. This process can take weeks or months."

"Let's say weeks."

"Okay, weeks, but what if we did everything possible to transform our culture? Let's start to show staff that we are taking action now."

"I like where you're going with this, Janni. I'm at the basketball game now and I'm running a bit late. Can you take a few minutes to send me your thoughts by email? I will review them tonight and then let's chat first thing tomorrow. We really need to get ahead of this thing."

Guy hung up the phone, jumped out of the car, and rushed to the basketball game. He thought through their conversation with Janni, the manager who just gave notice, and the others who had left in the previous months. He thought through the turnover rate and the concerns that had been raised in recent employee engagement surveys. *How do we fix this?*

He walked into the gym and quickly looked at the score board. His son's team was only down two points in the first quarter.

"That's a good thing," he said to himself as he took a seat at the back of the gym. Right now, the top priority was cheering on his son's team, so they could win the game.

CHAPTER 2:

The Retirement

"Tell me what you pay attention to and I will tell you who you are."
\- José Ortega y Gasset

"YOU'RE WHAT?"

Kathleen's response was loud and surprised the two gentlemen in the room.

"Yes, I think it's time for me to move on to the next phase of my life and hand over the reins of this company to the next person in line."

Kathleen couldn't believe what she was hearing. She knew Bill had made comments before about retiring to an Amish community somewhere out in the Milverton area, but she always thought it was just a joke. He had been such a great sponsor for her over the years and losing him was not something she was even considering right now.

"And yes, I am still moving to Milverton to start my new life of solitude," Bill said, with a smile on his face.

Both Kathleen and Marvin struggled to put a smile on their faces.

"The board and I have been talking about this for a few months now and we've decided on how we plan to revamp the organization."

Kathleen felt a bit uncomfortable having this conversation with Marvin in the room. Should this not be more of a one-on-one conversation? Shouldn't there be interviews for the leadership role? She knew she wasn't in line for the CEO role, and wasn't thinking about it either, but she was still uncomfortable.

She shook her head and pushed to refocus on the conversation.

"So, who is taking over from you?"

"Kathleen, I'd like you to meet the new CEO of TBO Bank."

Kathleen finally figured out why Marvin had been acting awkward since she had walked into Bill's office. Though she couldn't point out exactly what it was, she had noticed that he was a little more subdued than normal. She guessed that the board must have selected who they wanted before agreeing to announce Bill's retirement.

"Congratulations, Marvin. I'm really happy for you." Kathleen tried hard to be as genuine as possible.

"Thank you!" replied Marvin.

"Both of you will need to work a lot more closely to ensure we stay the course and take this organization to the next level. As you know, competition is tight, and this organization needs leaders with fresh ideas that can keep growing our asset base through strategic expansion and initiatives."

Both Kathleen and Marvin nodded in agreement.

"The rest of the executive team will be hearing from me about this today. Announcements will be shared with the rest of the company once the communications team have finished putting it together. Expect something out by next the week, so please keep this confidential."

"Bill, this is going to be a well-deserved break from all you have done over the years," Kathleen said, as she walked around his desk to give him a hug.

"Well, I'm just looking forward to not having the both of you chasing me down every day to be at meetings!" He smiled.

"Oh yeah, one more thing." Bill continued. 'I will be staying on to Chair the board. This still gives me a chance to influence things around here—from a distance, of course. The board chairman is also retiring, which has opened up this opportunity."

"Well, congratulations again! Thanks for letting me know."

Kathleen walked out of Bill's office shocked but hopeful. Marvin had worked at the executive level for various departments for a number of years. If there was someone to get this role, he was the one. But what did this mean for her, she wondered, as she headed back to her office.

Her office phone rang as soon as she stepped in.

"Hello, this is Kathleen."

"Hi Kathleen, Marvin here. You walked out before we could chat this through. Hope things are good?"

"Oh, yeah, I'm so sorry. I have a few key projects on the go, so I wanted to make sure I take some time to review a report before I head out for the day."

"Makes sense. I was calling to see if you would be available to meet sometime next week. Maybe over lunch or an early dinner? I want to get your thoughts on the organization and discuss how we can work with the rest of the leadership team to move the company forward."

"What exactly did you want my input on?"

"I'd like to have a sit-down conversation with you to start putting a plan in place ahead of moving to the new role. I would love to get your thoughts on what is missing and any specific projects you would like to focus on."

"Oh, okay. Hold on a second." Kathleen looked at her calendar. "Why don't we meet at Buantum on King Street for Monday evening. Say 4:00 p.m.?"

"Great, see you then."

C.O.O.

Kathleen walked into Buantum Monday evening not knowing what to expect. She'd been so busy over the past few days that she had not had any time to think about Bill's moving on and Marvin's promotion to CEO.

Both Kathleen and Marvin had never really had a problem working together. The key concern Kathleen had was how the dynamic would change as they adjusted to Marvin leading the organization. They were previously colleagues, but now she would be reporting to him.

She had so much on the go that she had not even thought about who the potential COO would be either. Had the board made their decision on what that could look like? Would this be open for interviews or would they select internally?

Rather than stress herself out with all her questions, Kathleen decided to commit to supporting the organization's choice, regardless of what direction they decided on.

"How may I help you?" A waiter brought Kathleen out of her trance.

"I'm so sorry; I'm here to meet with a colleague, Marvin."

"Ah, yes, he's in the back corner by the window. Please follow me."

As Kathleen walked up to the table, she saw Marvin on the phone. As soon as he saw her, he immediately wrapped up his conversation and stood to greet her.

"Hey, thanks for coming."

"No worries. How are you?"

"You know…the usual. It's been a busy day."

The waiter took their orders and headed off. Marvin held off conversation until the waiter was out of listening distance and then said, "I know you have a lot on the go, so I won't take up too much of your time."

"Thanks," Kathleen said, grateful that he was aware that she had to head home soon for family time with the kids.

"Kathleen, I've really enjoyed working with you over the past couple of years. From watching you lead the integration project for the merger with Aquilox Bank and also leading the restructuring of operations project, you have really impressed me with your ability to manage multiple projects and manage our people through change."

Kathleen thanked Marvin for his kind comments. This was the first time he had ever shared any of this with her.

"Another thing I really admire about you, Kathleen, is your ability to consistently present ideas or opportunities with a win-win message. I have noticed on a number of occasions how you spend time listening to others and always find ways to validate and incorporate their comments into your strategies. I've been here at TBO for almost 20 years now and honestly, I've not seen anyone connect with people the way you do."

"Thank you."

"I believe as we grow and create a new chapter at TBO, that kind of perspective and behaviour is going to be critical to our success."

The waiter arrived with their drinks and placed them on the table.

"We have some really big problems at TBO and I'd like to tackle them head on. Tackling them will push me head-to-head with some of our executive team and directors who have always thought "the culture is just the way it is." Bill and I have been talking about our plans for change and how to create a stronger position in the marketplace. And we are thinking how we interact— deliberately—will be a key part in this change process.

Kathleen nodded in agreement. Being a bank, TBO had always had a strong hierarchical style of management. Since Bill took over as the CEO of the organization 10 years ago, he had made some attempts to consciously work on the culture. But something always came up: the board was more concerned with profits; competition was going after one of their lines of business; or there were lots of changes happening at different levels of the organization chart. An even greater challenge to his efforts to create a collaborative culture was the fact that the bank had 150 branches, 300 managers, and just over 2,500 employees.

"So, with all that said, Bill and I are looking to have you join the leadership team as the new Chief Operating Officer."

Kathleen almost choked on her drink. "What? Wow! What!"

Marvin laughed quietly. He had been waiting for this moment and it was as shocking as he hoped it would be. "Now before you say no or think of that, I have asked the board for the freedom to build my own team. If they are looking for me to make an impact at TBO, they have agreed to step back a bit and support me as best as they can. They have also pushed me to ensure I work with the current team before trying to recruit anyone from outside."

"Wow. I'm…."

"Let me share a few thoughts around why I thought—actually, why Bill and I thought—you would be the best candidate."

Marvin was not going to give Kathleen a chance to say no.

"Kathleen, you love people. You are very passionate about people engagement. I've seen you interact with everyone from James and Ali in security, all the way up to Mina, who you know is always a handful. You genuinely show interest in who they are and their lives, you always want to add value. You are also very passionate about Marketing and Operations."

Kathleen was shocked. She controlled herself to smile professionally, but fireworks of excitement were going through her brain. She felt a sense of pride and gratefulness simultaneously.

"I knew Jane was going to be too busy to handle the culture transformation. In fact, when Jane and I spoke about this, we both felt you were next in line to handle this. With your background in marketing, your passion for operations, and ability to engage others, we felt that you have the right skills, mindset, and values needed to drive this change we're looking for."

Kathleen was not thinking of saying no at all. Moving up the ranks would be perfect at her current life stage. The kids were more independent now and she had found real satisfaction in being able to balance her work and life priorities.

"Okay, say no more," Kathleen jumped in with a smile on her face. She figured if she didn't, Marvin would continue trying to sell the new role to her. "My answer is yes. I would be honoured to join your team."

Marvin was thrilled to hear the good news. "Let's make a toast. To TBO and the future!"

Both laughed as they clinked their glasses together and took a drink. Kathleen had a lot of questions to ask but wanted to savour the moment.

"A key area I'd like you to focus on is transforming the culture of the organization."

Kathleen nodded and continued to listen.

"We are in a tough situation. Our employee engagement scores are at an all-time low across the board. Yes, there a few bright spots like in your department, but overall, they continue to trend in the wrong direction. HR has been making it known that it is getting harder to compete to find top talent because we have low ratings on various hiring websites, and when they investigate, more than 69 per cent of the claims are true. Since our recent two acquisitions, it seems we have a company of six different cultures trying to figure out how to work as one. Let us not even go into our turnover rate—our exit interviews are making it evident that we have some work to do. If we do not figure out how to fix this, Kathleen, we are nothing more than a sinking ship."

The drive home was a time of reflection for Kathleen. As a director, she had noticed how her direct reports had sometimes spoken to their team members and she never liked it. She had noticed there was an underlying *command and control* culture with managers exerting authority on staff members. It was subtle but was obvious. And it seemed like some managers knew this was not what she wanted, so either they had stopped it or not done it in front of her. The culture at TBO was a problem, but Kathleen had never seen it as something she could solve, especially since her group's scores were always high, and HR had rarely approached her with any concerns. In her opinion, she was not the CEO or VP of Human Resources.

Kathleen had more questions than answers, but for the rest of the drive home, she just wanted to enjoy the moment. She turned on the radio and smiled to herself. Kathleen, COO.

ROUGH SLEEP

Guy rushed to get ready for work. He normally had an exercise routine every morning but he had to skip it so he could get to work on time. When he walked into the kitchen, his wife Theresa was already there getting her morning coffee ready.

"Are we still on for our date this evening, Mister?"

"You bet! Looking forward to it. How are you?"

"I'm good," Theresa said, with a smile on her face as she sipped her coffee.

"Alyssa! Rashon! Hurry up so you don't miss your bus. Breakfast is ready," yelled Theresa as both kids slowly walked down the stairs mumbling.

"Did you have a rough sleep last night? I noticed you got up a few times through the night."

"I just have some work issues on my mind."

"Anything I can help with?" Theresa asked.

"No. I will get it sorted out shortly. I also had the last slice of pizza in the fridge," Guy said smiling. "So that probably did not help either."

"So that's where the final slice went. I thought it was Alyssa." Rashon looked disappointed at the news as he went through his backpack to make sure he had all his stuff for school.

"Please have something to eat this morning, Alyssa," her mom said as she grabbed her laptop bag for work. "And Rashon, tonight is basketball practice, and I have already asked Daniel's mom to drive you. So please be ready."

As she walked to the door leading out to the driveway, she whispered into Guy's ear, "Looking forward to our night out tonight, honey." She winked at Guy and smiled.

"Oh, by the way, I am speaking at the Board of Trade meeting this afternoon. So, I should be home by 6:30."

"Oh great. What are you speaking about?"

"How Savos stayed lean during the 2009 financial crisis. And there will be another speaker after me talking about culture change, I think."

"Nice. Well, good luck and do not be late."

"See you tonight, love." Guy gave his wife a kiss as she walked out of the house. He then turned to see if his kids were ready for him to drop them off at school. He laughed to himself thinking about the culture speaker—these guys always tell you the same thing.

CHAPTER 3:

The Seed

"Change will not come if we wait for some other person, or if we wait for some other time. We are the ones we've been waiting for. We are the change that we seek."
- Barack Obama

GUY ARRIVED AT Savos headquarters just after 7:30 a.m. He had come in early to go through some reports, prepare for his many meetings, and to make sure that he had plenty of time to review his presentation for the Board of Trade meeting.

As he was walking towards the elevator, his cell phone rang. It was Janni.

"Hey, Janni, please don't give me any bad news this morning."

"Ha-ha, nothing bad this morning."

Guy gave a big sigh and then said, "Thanks for your email last night. And I completely agree—we need to get all area directors on a call to discuss this union issue. Can you make that happen for this Friday? I want to make sure they are well informed."

"Will do. I will also send them some information about rules of engagement when it comes to unions."

"Any update from the labour union?"

"Well, we still won't hear anything until after approval from the labour board. It's only been a day, Guy."

"No news is good news!" Guy replied with enthusiasm. "I'm very concerned about this, Janni. Let's meet this afternoon with Ari from Legal to ensure we stay ahead of this."

"Sure thing, Guy. Are you at the office already?"

"The early bird eats the best worms! Where are you?"

"Still having breakfast."

"Ha-ha, enjoy your morning with the family. Say hi to Felicia for me. See you later."

Guy hung up the phone as he pushed the button for the elevator. The elevator door opened, and as he walked in, a young lady walked in after him.

She pushed the button for the 10th floor. Savos leased all the floors between 10th and 16th, with two of the floors sharing office space with other organizations, but the 10th floor was all Savos. The departments for regional operations, process improvements, food safety and services, supplier relations, and restaurant décor. He knew she worked for Savos, but did not know for which department. Nevertheless, he was slightly embarrassed that he didn't know who she was.

Guy knew that for him to change the culture, he would have to be different. He would personally have to be more connected to what they were doing. He decided to take the first step, no matter how uncomfortable it was going to feel.

"Good morning. Guy Topper."

"Good morning. Ravi Gil."

"Forgive me for asking, but what department do you work in? I apologize for not knowing."

"I'm with Process Improvement. This is a company of over 2,000 people. I'm sure, as president, it would be impossible for you to remember everyone's name and department. It's okay."

"Well, my new month resolution is to do my best to get to know the people working at Savos better, regardless of how many there are. So, I was wondering if you would be available to have lunch together and talk about the organization?"

"Um, sure. That should be okay," Ravi stammered. Guy could see he had surprised her with his request.

"I will have Sara, my assistant, email you later to confirm the time with you. And please… do not worry. My intent is not to put you off guard. I have realized that I am always rushing around to meetings when I should be rushing around to meet the people who work here more often."

Although he was doing his best to reassure her, he could only imagine the thoughts she'd have when she got to her department this morning.

When the elevator opened on the 10th floor, Ravi said, "Have a great day," and walked out.

Kathleen arrived at the Board of Trade lunch meeting just in time for the first speaker to take the stage. She recognized him from the award ceremony a month ago. With the official announcement of becoming the new COO at TBO, Kathleen had really struggled to find time to come to this month's luncheon. But from the request of Marvin to represent him, she felt the need to be there.

Guy Topper was the first of the two luncheon speakers. He told a great story about how his organization had evolved from one restaurant in Milton, Ontario, to a network of 100 locations across Canada. Kathleen was impressed by how Guy's focus on staying lean helped the company survive the hard times. She was impressed, but concerned, at what that kind of focus had on the customer and employee experience. Regardless, she was glad she was able to hear his speech.

After the emcee thanked Guy and shared association updates with the audience, there was a 10-minute break before the second speaker would be introduced. Every time she came to these events, she could not help but laugh to herself when she saw all the executives put their heads down and go right to their phones instead of networking—like the event was meant for.

She walked over to Guy as he headed back to his seat. "That was an impressive story, thanks for sharing."

"Oh, Merci!"

"Your Savos story required a lot of doggedness to make it through the rough times between years five and seven."

"You're right. But it seems doggedness was required at every stage of the journey. We have new battles to face today, and we have to face them head on."

They were chatting more about some of Guy's insights about growing the company when the emcee called the room back to order and asked everyone to take their seats.

Kathleen exchanged contact information with Guy and went back to her seat. She was pleased with the first speaker and was ready to hear more.

"Our next speaker has been studying and researching the human side of business operations since high school. He has lived in Canada for most of his life but has a world view like no other. Lately he has been spending time researching and writing and working with leaders in different organizations to help them transform their culture—both from a conscious and collaborative perspective. Everyone, please help me welcome the founder of The Culture Zone, Mr. Derek Owoson!"

Derek stood up from his seat at one of the front tables, smiled, waved to the audience, and walked up on stage. He shook hands with the emcee and then walked to the centre of the stage, looked over the audience, and then quietly said, "I want to start with this core statement…and whether you agree with it or not, I'd like you to really think about it. **Your company culture is the DNA of your organization's success.** *Get the culture right, then everything else that you need to be successful will fall into place.*"

Derek left a long pause so everyone could let the words sink in. He continued, "How important is culture? Take a moment and consider these numbers:"

Businesses must invest in their workplace culture, developing a clear set of values on which to base practices, and reviewing these policies as the company grows and develops, according to employers (96 per cent) and professionals (98 per cent) alike.[i]

In the USA and Canada, 55 per cent of the workforce is not engaged and 15 per cent are actively disengaged. That means 510 out of 1,000 of these employees are just getting by.[ii]

91 per cent of U.S. managers say culture fit is more important than experience or skills. [iii]

Positive culture is a vital aspect of running a business—more than 50 per cent of executives say corporate culture influences productivity, creativity, profitability, firm value, and growth rates.[iv]

Over the next 30 minutes, Derek wowed the audience with stories of organizations who ignored their cultural thermometer or had poor cultures—consciously or unconsciously—creating a ripple effect that ultimately impacted employee motivation, turnover, revenue, market share, and innovation. He shared incredible stories about leaked memos, executive sabotage, and confidential documents shared with the media. One company had the executive team place trackers in the CEO's car and office, so they could know what he was planning. That story left the entire room in stitches.

To ensure his message was heard, he left the stage and walked around the room to connect better with his audience. As Derek talked about the impact of culture on the entire organization's overall success, Kathleen could not help but think about her conversation with Marvin and the culture at TBO. How could she have missed so much of this ever since she joined the organization?

Derek continued. "It is often said that an organization's culture can most simply be thought of as "the way things are done around here". But in these times of constant change it is **more** than that. Much more than that. Culture is like DNA. We can see without the most powerful microscope, but we all are very confident in our belief that it exists. Culture is who we are based on the millions of little factors and events that have happened to us and are happening to us – all the time. Even right now." The room became very quiet as Derek's words drew the attention of everyone in the room.

"At the Culture Zone, we have done extensive research on successful organizations. We have met with their CEOs, Chief People Leaders, sat with frontline staff members, and spent hours interviewing, observing, and collecting data. We have also interviewed and met with others who have changed cultures outside of the corporate world. We've learned so much about culture and have seen so many recurring patterns. Through all of this, we have been able to create a model that can help transform your culture."

Derek took a long pause that drew everyone in as he walked back to the front of the room. "Our formula is what we call the Culture Ring—four distinct phases of transformation that help organizations create desired cultures—effectively and efficiently." For the first time in the 30 minutes, he had been speaking, he pointed the attendees' attention to the screen. And on cue, the Culture Ring diagram appeared.

The Culture Ring©

As he spoke, a few members of the audience lifted their smartphones to take a picture.

"The words in the boxes are not new to any of you here today, but what is new is how we combine each aspect to bring about cultural transformation, quickly. Let me tell you about each phase."

"The foundation of transformation begins with getting a clear picture of who you are. Who you are as individuals and as well as an organization. We call this phase **The Culture Identity.** Even though culture may not be immediately observable, identifying a set of values is always helpful in terms of measuring and managing culture more effectively. As you know, culture is based on attitudes, beliefs, customs, and rules - written and unwritten - that have been in place over a period of time. And all of these aspects lead to the values that promote behaviours and create your culture. Our *Values. Culture. Period* Assessment has the empirical research to help you learn about, leverage and transform or reinforce your cultural identity."

Guy could not believe what he was hearing. The speaker was talking exactly about what Savos was facing. He looked around the room and nobody looked back at him. Everyone was looking at and listening to what Derek was sharing. Others were opening laptops and were taking notes while some in the back were standing up and taking pictures of the speaker with their smartphones.

"What excites me the most about assessing and identifying the culture is that it allows you to become very intentional about different parts of your culture and keep your eye on your culture thermometer."

"Phase two—"***Operational Values Model***, or OVM, builds on the 'what' from the culture identity and assessment of values and focuses on 'where'. Where do you start to make values you want and the culture you desire come to life? The OVM phase is where the work gets more challenging because it involves three key perspectives or lenses for implementation: strategic imperatives, learning methodologies and process navigation. The OVM provides a process to embed values into your daily organization operations."

"This phase is challenging but rewarding, because you can use the values you have, or re-write the genetic code of your organization. For all of you science lovers out there – you know how cool that would be." Derek smiled as many in the audience laughed at his comment.

Derek continued. "The third area is development. But I want you to think deeper about what development means. My research has shown me that it comes from the 1600s French word *développer*, and originally meant to **unroll or unfold.** The mindset we need in this third phase is just that—we need to unfold and make apparent the potential in our performers, at all levels. And that development must begin with ***leadership development***. But intentional development at all levels —frontline, middle managers and then your executive team."

Many in the audience were now nodding their heads in agreement or were making more notes on the laptops or pads of paper.

"Are you aware that employees who rate their managers poorly are four times more likely to interview for other positions when compared to their peers? Personal and team leadership development, from a cultural perspective, ensures that everyone understands their role in building a great culture. It also allows culture transformation to happen faster because everyone is on the same page. You cannot embed your values, improve employee engagement, and transform your culture but not work on the mindset of leaders at every level."

"The last phase is about making culture stick —real engagement, or as we call it ***values engagement.*** This phase is essential to pulling all your insights and conversations together to sustain the transformation. We are living in the experience economy, so we need to create an experience that drives engagement. Engagement with team and employee values. You are all familiar with the term *employee engagement*, which is the extent to which employees feel passionate about their work and are committed to your organization. Value engagement is the consistent process of ensuring values at all levels of the organization are aligned. You cannot change your culture if your employees' values are not considered or aligned."

"Our work has shown us that you cannot have a culture that *you want*, if you do not have strong, *active values in place*. Values that dictate the behaviours you celebrate and communicate consistently. Your values determine the key outputs in your culture."

Derek then took a step towards the audience, leaned forward, and said, "Or worse, if the values are aligned with behaviours that are in opposition to business goals."

"In closing, if you want to drive business results for the long haul, consider how seriously you take culture. And remember this number, 55 per cent. Fifty-five per cent of the current work force is engaged. What would it mean to your business if we increased that to 75 per cent or 85 per cent, ideally 100 per cent? My name is Derek, and it has been a pleasure being a part of your culture today."

Derek rounded up his speech to a resounding applause. The emcee walked up to the stage to thank Derek for his insights and tools and give his final remarks.

While the emcee was sharing final thoughts on the two speakers and Board business, Kathleen could not put her finger on it, but something just did not sit with her. The information seemed relevant, the stories and statistics credible…but somehow, she did not buy into it.

"What did you think?" A voice from behind Kathleen caught her off guard. It was Guy.

"About what?

"About the ring and the VMO stuff. What Derek just spoke about?"

"Well…" Kathleen said unenthusiastically. "It seems like he had the research to back up his ideas, but I'm not sure that stuff would work in our industry. I'm in banking, and banking will always need to manage the values of our shareholder, government policies, and customers. There are too many players involved for us to pick a few values to run our business through. I cannot really put my finger on it, but I was not fully convinced."

"Interesting… what about it wasn't convincing?"

"I'm not really sure, Guy. I'm not really into soft things. I've always had issues with people like this who make these speeches. They have never run a multinational company before or had to deal with shareholders, stock market, and other complexities around running a large organization. Their firm is usually about 5–10 people and they want to consult for a company of 700–10,000? It doesn't make sense."

Guy was silent.

"Well, what do you think?" Kathleen asked, noticing Guy's silence.

"You are right about your concern, but I do think it is important to keep in mind that people like Derek have spent a lot of time focused on doing the in-depth research and studies. This is their area of expertise. Yours is managing a financial business, mine is working in the restaurant industry, and theirs is building cultures. You do not ask them to come run your company for you. I look at them like surgeons, who have spent a lot of time in a specific part of business—and an area where very few ever spend time thinking about, much less getting right."

"You are right, actually. What were your thoughts on the speech though?"

"I thought it was excellent. We are currently facing a major challenge. There have been some rumblings from employees about bringing a union into Savos. We are looking for a solution that could work and quite frankly, I am all good with Derek being a team of seven or 70—if he has a solution that has been developed through research and practice, I definitely want to hear more and see if it can work for us."

"So, you are going to fall for that sales pitch?" Kathleen said, with a smile on her face.

Guy smiled back. "I like to think that I am going **buy** his solutions. I will do my due diligence, but he has done a great job of combining both the people and performance aspects of business. And honestly, Kathleen, our culture needs some work. I guess you and the TBO team have a very strong corporate culture?"

Kathleen smiled, picked up her glass of water, took a sip and then lied, "We are doing okay."

They chatted for another minute and then said their goodbyes. Kathleen then walked towards the Board President to introduce herself and apologize for Marvin not being able to make it.

LUNCH

Guy arrived at lunch not sure what to expect at his meeting with Ravi. He usually spent time outside the office having lunch with potential clients, current clients, or a member of the executive team. He was ashamed he had never really spent time getting to know staff members in the organization. Now he felt he had no choice. The clock was ticking, and they needed to know how to turn things around. "I need to lead by example," he repeatedly whispered to himself.

He arrived one minute late to the office cafeteria and noticed Ravi was already there eating. He grabbed a sandwich and a bottle of water, paid, and then walked over to Ravi's table.

"Sorry to keep you waiting."

"Nothing to worry about. I thought you got held up in meetings."

"I had a meeting that ran over time. I couldn't jump out. But no excuse, I apologize for keeping you waiting."

"That's fine. Well, you know what they say about bosses, don't you?"

"No, what do they say," asked Guy.

Ravi chuckled. "I'm not sure it is appropriate to be sharing this type of joke with the President."

Guy laughed out loud. "Oh…now I really have to hear it."

"A boss is like a diaper, always on your ass and usually full of…."

Ravi couldn't complete the sentence without laughing. "I'm so sorry, this is just so not appropriate." Guy joined her in laughing.

"That is one I will have to remember," Guy said as he started in on his lunch.

Guy continued the conversation by getting to know his Process Improvement employee more—her role, her team, and her interests. He asked about her passions, life, and family. Towards the end of lunch, he was still not sure how to get to the point. He was not even sure what point he was really trying to approach.

He decided to go for it. "Million-dollar question for you. Are you happy working at Savos?"

Ravi sat back and took her time to think about her response. "Yes, it is good," she said, trying hard to be convincing.

"Okay, let me put it this way. If you had a magic wand and had a chance to change anything in this organization, what would it be?"

"That's a tough question to answer, Mr. Topper."

"Pretend you could answer that question. If you knew the answer, what would you say? And whatever you say stays with me. You have my word."

Ravi took a long pause and sighed. She then spoke up. "I think we need to develop our managers more. Especially on how to appreciate and respect their people."

Ravi's tone immediately changed when she spoke those words. Her tone went from positive and energetic to measured and reserved. It seemed Guy had somehow hit a soft spot. He could feel the stress in her words.

"I'm so sorry, something difficult must have happened." Guy wasn't sure how to pull the information out, but he wanted to hear it.

"I appreciate my manager a lot. A whole lot…but I am tired of going home stressed and scared for my job. I cannot take it anymore." Ravi started to tear up.

Guy wasn't sure what to say or do. "I'm so sorry, Ravi."

She took the napkin off her tray to wipe her tears. Guy immediately handed her another one.

"I am not throwing my manager under the bus, and I apologize if I am."

"Why haven't you reported any of this before? Maybe to your team director or someone in human resources?"

"Report a manager at Savos? I do not think so." And she wiped another tear from the corner of her eye and then adjusted her glasses.

"The problem is not the reporting. The problem is the retaliation after the reporting. It is subtle, it is covert, but it happens. At least that is what I have heard from others. People have just learned to shut their mouths, do their work, and try to stay under the radar."

Guy felt like he had just been slapped in the face. If this was how employees were feeling at head office, no wonder there were union conversations happening at the restaurants. Guy wanted to get to the bottom of this.

"What else have you noticed about how other employees are feeling? I don't need names, just what have you seen?"

"If you come down here to lunch regularly, you will be shocked by the number of people complaining daily. Yes, work is getting done and people collaborate, but it feels forced all the time."

Guy felt bad. How had he missed this all along? How come he had never taken his time to talk to his people to understand their pain-points? But he knew why. He had been too busy working on the organization, concerned about the stakeholders, and his own agenda rather than giving appropriate time to the employees' agenda. It was horrible that it took a union drive to wake him up to the people side of the business.

"I assure you, we will be doing something about this, and I'm sorry you and others have had these experiences here, Ravi. Sorry to hear you've gone through this."

Guy stood up and thanked her for her time. He empathized with her. She must have felt relief, but also embarrassment and fear, after sharing her story with him.

Ravi started to tidy up her tray. "I have to head back now for a team meeting as well. Thank you for inviting me to lunch and I apologize for my tears."

"I hope I am not a diaper at all."

Ravi couldn't help but start laughing. It made her feel a lot better knowing that the president of Savos was able to take a good joke and remember it.

As Guy walked away towards the elevator, he pulled out his phone and called Sara.

"Hey, Sara, please book time for me to meet with Janni later today. And can you also please call Derek Owoson from the Culture Zone? I'd like him to come in to meet with Janni and me as soon as possible."

"Sure thing, Guy," said Sara.

Guy put the phone in his pocket and walked into the elevator. Another employee walked in behind him.

"Hi, I'm Guy, your CEO and diaper."

"Diaper?" The employee said, looking confused.

"Well, you know what they say, CEOs are like diapers."

The elevator door shut as they both laughed and started chatting.

CHANGE

It was mid-December in Toronto. The air was buzzing with the feeling of Christmas fast approaching. Christmas lights were up everywhere and there was an extra level of cheer in the air. The festive sense was here.

Kathleen always loved the festive season. As a child, Christmas was always a special time for her and the family. Coming from a divorced home, she always cherished the holiday period, because after the divorce, both of her parents agreed to always spend Christmas morning together, as a way of sharing the special time with the kids.

Although Kathleen and her siblings sometimes felt a little tension in the air, they always enjoyed having Dad over right after breakfast. Opening presents was always a delight. It seemed that both Mom and Dad always tried to subtly outdo each other every year. Kathleen and her siblings loved this; it meant they all got great presents.

Sadly, Kathleen had not been able to replicate this for her children with her ex-husband. Though Christmas was an amazing time in the city, in Kathleen's personal life, it also brought on occasional feelings of regret and nostalgia. Despite her feelings around the holiday, she was glad that at TBO, Christmas was a time of joy and appreciation. It helped take away the moody Christmas moments for her.

Kathleen walked into the boardroom at 9:53 a.m. to join the rest of the executives. The meeting started at 10 a.m. It was an hour she would forever remember.

Marvin kicked off the meeting asking Lily, from the Continuous Improvement Team, for an update on the latest process improvements for the Mortgage Loan Process Project.

"We are at the 3rd phase of the project and I am happy to say we are right on target," Lily said confidently. "We have a few major milestones we're aiming for over the next six weeks, but I believe the needs analysis, mapping stage, and risk assessments have been extremely successful. We will begin creating a transition and communication plan and work with IT to finalize and implement software upgrade strategies. Phase 4 commences next month."

Kathleen chimed in, "Lily and I are pushing to ensure we leave no person or department behind through this reformation process."

"We'll be having an update meeting in five days with more details. You all should have already received the calendar invitation in your email," Lily added.

"Thank you, Lily. I appreciate the depth of work you and the team have put into this process improvement update," Marvin said. "Saul, can you run us through our numbers for this quarter?"

"Absolutely, Marvin. Merry Christmas to all you elves."

The group chuckled a bit. Saul was the office comedian, joker, and a great VP of Sales.

"Well, we've been good boys and girls at TBO, and Santa has been good to us. It's looking like we'll surpass our targeted revenue for this year by 22 per cent."

The good news filled the room with positive energy. A few members clapped while Saul stood up and took a bow. Everyone in the room laughed.

"Fifty per cent of our revenue came from an area of the business that we had projected would lose significance in the customer's eye in the next five years, but that's okay. We will take that win for today. In the next quarter, my team will be looking closely at the various market categories to determine where and how to diversify our sales and service products going forward."

"That is really encouraging, Saul. Thank you. We will make time at our next retreat to look closer at future revenue streams and how we want to position ourselves for the future," Marvin replied, stopping Saul from diving into another series of witty comments.

"Jane, what do you have for us from HR?"

Jane cleared her throat, looked around the room slowly, and said, "I want to start out by first saying we are in a crisis mode at TBO."

That caught the attention of the entire room.

"What do you mean?" asked Gerald, VP of Banking Services.

"Based on some of the reports we have been pulling, our engagement scores have dropped significantly, and our turnover numbers are rising fast.

Our turnover—when totalling averages from the 13 business units—has risen by another 10 per cent over the past quarter. If you compare the figures over the previous four quarters, you will see a steady increase. It is significantly larger than last year's numbers for the same time period. Something is going wrong, and we are not addressing it."

"Well, if there is something going wrong, I would expect HR to know what that is," said Mina, the VP of IT.

It seemed either that Jane did not hear her or pretended not to hear her.

Straight-faced and focused on her presentation, Jane said, "From the information we are gathering, especially from exit interviews, it seems staff members are having poor relations with their managers, but they are not speaking up."

"Jane, I do not understand. Why have we not started diving in and starting to have conversations with these directors and managers who are losing staff? Would that not have been a natural solution for HR to run with?" Mina asked, with a bit of frustration in her voice.

"Mina, in HR, our goal is to empower all staff to communicate effectively. It is not my team's job to tell your managers how to work with their staff. I am sure you are aware of that," Jane replied directly, and addressing Mina head on.

"Hey, everyone, please," said Marvin. "We are all on the same team. We are trying to solve the same problem." Marvin felt the tension rising in the room.

Both ladies turned to face Marvin.

Marvin looked around the room to ensure he had everyone's attention. "Jane, thanks for bringing this to our attention. Let's you, Mina and I connect after this meeting to discuss what we can do regarding this issue. How does that sound?"

Both Jane and Mina nodded their heads in agreement.

"Great," Marvin said, feeling good that he had averted an argument. "Okay, team, so I have an announcement I need to share with everyone that I think will help us understand where we are today and where we are looking to go. The board presented an idea that I'd like us to discuss as well."

"Which basically means we have to do it," chimed Saul, in a light-hearted and sarcastic tone.

Marvin continued. "As you know, as an organization, the board has recognized and agreed that we will be moving into growth mode and aiming to double our branch size over the next five years. One of the quickest ways we can do this is through acquisitions. We have been given approval to look at some smaller banks in medium-sized communities that have strong assets we can bring under the TBO umbrella. Potential acquisitions to start with before thinking of mergers. Our legal team has been doing some preliminary work in that area and we have found a few banks that we could start negotiating with."

"Well, come on with it. We want to hear who these companies are," Saul said. He was too excited to hold his breath any longer. Everyone in the room laughed at Saul's enthusiasm.

"Billings?" Marvin looked at Keon, Head of Legal, who stood up and walked over to the boardroom's TV monitor to guide the group through his presentation slides.

Keon's first slide showed a list of 20 companies with their logo and their customer base size. "Right now, we have not fully firmed up the companies we will be working with, but as you can see, we are going to start with these 20, with our goal of getting down to five by the end of Q1 next year, and then proceed to make our first acquisition by the end of Q3. We want to take our time with this and speed up as we move to the end of the year."

Keon forwarded the slide to show the list of banks that TBO was going to focus on.

"Our first target on the list is Covenant Bank located in the town of Caledon. We love the number of accounts they have acquired over the past few years and the number of assets they currently own. We also know they are currently struggling as a few of the big commercial banks are coming into the local market to compete. They are looking for a top dog to come in to help pick them up."

"And here we are to the rescue," Kathleen said.

"We also have our eyes on Belville in Eastern Ontario. A few cannabis companies are close to opening in that area and we want to make sure we are there as population growth follows. Especially with the migration that should accompany what is going to be happening in that town. Elevation Bank is the number one bank we are looking at in that area."

Marvin jumped in. "Thanks, Keon. Keon and the team have also been working with Jane on some research around what makes mergers and acquisitions fail. I need to verify this, but I believe the stats say that 80 per cent of these things fail, and I want to make sure we do not. As you can imagine, there are several reasons why this happens. But having gone through one in my life before TBO, I know one of the biggest reasons is bad cultural integration. And that leads me to why I brought this up after Jane's feedback."

People in the room could tell where this was going.

"It is not news to any of us that our culture is not where we want it to be—case in point, Jane's comments earlier. If we are looking to bring in five companies over the next two years and doubling our number over five years, we need to figure out what our culture is, so we are in a position to smoothly integrate those of the banks we bring on."

Kathleen could now understand that Marvin was making culture transformation a priority. It was all coming together.

"So, what is the board suggesting about this cultural change?" asked Gerald.

"Well, they aren't giving suggestions, but more of a mandate. We have seen the numbers and I know that culture needs to be a focus as we grow. While Keon and his team keep continue sorting out the legal steps required and working with the marketing department to track day-to-day economic conditions in these communities, I am tasking Kathleen and Jane to start focusing on culture. We are going in this direction and we must get this right."

"Actually, my team is very busy right now, Marvin," Jane insisted. "We are very busy with the onboarding revamp and hiring process needed for the Mortgage Loan Process Improvement. I know we had discussed this a few weeks ago, but my team will not be able to give this the attention required right now. Kathleen, do you mind taking this on yourself? I can support from the sidelines and meet when you need me."

"Sure, we can do that," Kathleen replied hesitantly, concerned what this would mean if Human Resources was not more involved. After all, isn't culture really an HR problem, she thought.

"Marvin, what do you mean by focus on culture?" Mina looked confused.

Marvin paused for a moment, and then said, "Our turnover is high. Managers are not connecting with their team members as they should be, employee engagement scores are consistently moving in the wrong direction, and we are doing more hiring externally than internally just to keep up. If we cannot fix our own house, we are going to be in trouble when we bring on new entities. We will fail, and quite frankly if we fail, the board might start looking at some other options. Failure is not an option for our team."

The room finally understood the urgency of this request.

Mina first broke the silence, never ready to back down from a crucial conversation. "That really sounded like a threat, Marvin."

"That was not a threat, Mina. The board has identified this as the number one priority for the next three to five years. They are also under pressure to have everything lined up to present to interested and potential shareholders. If we fail with these acquisitions and subsequent mergers, I'm sure shareholders will start looking at fresh blood on the executive team. That will probably start with me."

Some in the room looked at each other blankly, while others started to make notes on their pads of paper in front of them.

"Okay, well, let's not get too uptight about this. I think we can do this," Saul said and then scanned the room to see who was with him. From his scan, it appeared that most in the room were unsure about his idea. "Santa has been good to us, in terms of reaching and exceeding our goals, and in terms of assets and revenue for this quarter. If we can do that, then surely we can turn this ship around."

"But how can we fix this, and where is Kathleen supposed to begin?" Saul asked and looked in her direction.

Suddenly, it all came back to Kathleen. The Board of Trade luncheon— the culture conversation, and the speaker who had shared the interesting concept about culture transformation. What did he call it? Oh yes, The Ring. But she was sceptical if his ideas would work in their industry.

But now, that did not seem to matter, Kathleen and her colleagues' careers were on the line.

"I have an idea, everyone. I was at a trade event this time last year," she said, "and a speaker had come in to talk about how to transform the culture of an organization. He shared some really great ideas and I know the person sitting next to me had mentioned his company will be working with the speaker."

"Great! Call his ass now!" Saul chimed in with all the enthusiasm in the world. The room burst out in laughter.

"Kathleen, please, let's reach out. I want you to take the lead on this. Spring is right around the corner, so let's make this happen. Keon, we are hoping to get more details on the 10 companies and what the potential timeline would be. Let's work together to have that ready for the team next week," Marvin shared.

Keon acknowledged Marvin's request as he shut down the presentation. "Great work, everyone. I'll see you all at next week's huddle."

Kathleen was known for always arriving early for meetings, but having to lead the culture change and preparing for expansion these past few weeks were making her start to feel the pressure. Meetings were coming back-to-back and there was little wiggle room to arrive at the next meeting before it started.

She hurried into the meeting and quickly took her seat, whispering a sorry to Gerald.

Gerald stood. "Okay, let's get started."

It was the monthly branch manager's meeting with managers from across the region. Kathleen would normally not attend these meetings, but with the Mortgage Loan Process reaching its 3rd phase, the managers needed to be informed on where the project was and the proposed changes that would affect their teams.

"Hi, everyone, I want to first say a big congratulations to you all for a great sales effort this quarter. Kudos to you and your sales team for a job well done."

There were some nods in the room and people looked at one another smiling.

"Let's take a look at some of our key numbers from the month, shall we?" Marvin said. "Gerald, the floor is yours."

Gerald and his team had spent time going through key scorecards from the month. The managers identified wins and areas of opportunity for them to discuss. They also dived into how things were going in their branches.

When it was Kathleen's turn to lead the meeting, she walked the group through the proposed changes. She also took time answering questions and clarifying responsibilities for the group.

Gerald thanked Kathleen for her time and continued the meeting. As the meeting was coming close to ending, it happened.

Terry Green, one of the Branch Managers from the Montreal area, spoke up over the phone and asked a question, "Gerald, there is an issue with one of the legacy staff members at my branch. They are refusing to even hear some of the changes we are proposing around training new staff members."

"I know this is not easy for all of them, but it is your job to get them on board, Green," said Gerald. "They have received more than enough lead time to know what is happening and why. Let them know this is not negotiable."

Gerald tried to sound tactful, but the tone was impatient. Kathleen knew he had been under a lot of stress lately.

"If you cannot figure out how to get them onboard, then I may have to come down there and show you how to do it. And that goes for everyone."

The silence filled the room. Kathleen couldn't believe her ears.

"Any more questions?" Gerald asked.

No one dared ask any other questions.

Gerald thanked Kathleen once again for her time and closed out the meeting.

Kathleen walked out very concerned. The need for a culture change was clear.

It was a cold Thursday afternoon in mid-January, a year after Guy and the team had implemented the Culture Transformation Program at Savos. Kathleen, COO at TBO, walked into Dinein Coffee early for her meeting with Guy. She had brought her laptop, so she could have at least 30 minutes to get some work done before the meeting.

"Dark roast coffee, please. Large."

"What would you like with your coffee?" asked the waiter.

"Nothing else at the moment, thank you."

Kathleen sat back for a moment and started to think about how she would approach the conversation. She wasn't sure how to start, but felt it would be good to get an idea of what had worked for Guy at Savos.

"Looks like you got here early to get some work done." A voice with a Quebecois accent came from behind her as she typed away on her laptop.

Guy was 10 minutes earlier than expected.

"Oh, hey. Yes, I wanted to get some work done out of the office. How are you?"

"Très bien! How were your holidays?" Guy pulled off his jacket as he took a seat across from Kathleen.

"It was great. The kids and I had a really great time. And, of course, we all ate way too much."

"Ha-ha. The same with us. Lots of food too."

After the waiter had taken Guy's order, Guy leaned forward in his chair and said, "So you mentioned on the phone you wanted to discuss the Ring. I'm really interested in knowing why. Last time we had spoken, you weren't really impressed by it."

"Yes, you're right. I must admit, I was probably a little…"

"A little bit or a big-time-doubter?" Guy smiled.

"Okay. I deserved that. You are right. I really never gave it a chance. But now I'm interested in learning more about how it is working at Savos."

Guy took a long pause as he sipped his coffee. He looked out the coffee shop window like he was searching for a place to begin. Kathleen almost looked out as well, trying to figure out what he was staring at. Then he spoke.

"It's been a year since we started the journey. Let's say, with the scare of staff members signing the union card, we had to make changes and we had very little time to do it."

"So how did you go about it? What did you learn? Did it work? What were some issues that came up?"

Guy laughed hysterically as Kathleen bombarded him with questions.

"Whoa! I cannot give you all the secrets. If you want to make this simple, I suggest you do one thing before the end of the day: give Derek a call. I will give you this assurance: if you really want to turn your culture around, he and his team have the right experience and tools for you."

"How did you know it was the right program?" Kathleen asked.

"I was so desperate that anything would have been right for me. But when we started to discuss the questions he asked us such as *what our organization was really about*, it became very clear to me, and several in the room, that we needed to make big changes."

Kathleen leaned forward with raised eyebrows. "So, what did you do?"

"As the leader of the team, I realized that I had been playing it safe. It was time to make some really tough decisions and start to show up. We had to have some tough conversations and had to switch some people's areas of focus. It was very challenging at the onset and for most of the journey, but the more we looked at ourselves, the more we realized this was what we needed to do."

"How did you know it was the right "experience" for you?"

"It was only our second session with Derek and his direct question of each of the leadership team members really got us thinking about what we were trying to achieve at Savos. Why were all of us in the roles we were in? He made us think about what we mean and represent to our customers."

"What do you mean?"

"You won't really understand until you take the journey," Guy said with a smile. "But I think there was a point at that meeting where every leader had to make a choice between jumping on the new train of unchartered territory or hanging on to their old self."

Kathleen spent a few seconds to take in what Guy was saying.

Guy continued, "Reach out to Derek and have a conversation with him. A lot of things that I could tell you won't make much sense right now. It will make a lot more sense coming from him."

They continued to talk about their companies for another 20 minutes and then Kathleen thanked Guy for his time. Though she wanted to know more about Derek and his process, she felt she got what she needed to make her decision.

Guy got up and started to put on his jacket. "Kathleen, are you sure your team is ready for this? I suggest you check in with them first. The Ring is very revealing. Don't move forward if you are not ready. It's going to take honesty, humility, and hard work."

Kathleen walked out of the coffee shop and decided to give the Ring a chance. But Guy was right—was her team ready for this? She was. Marvin was. But what about the rest of the leadership? What about the organization as a whole?

As she walked back to the office, her phone buzzed. She swiped it opened and saw that it was a text from Guy, with Derek's phone number. She stopped in the middle of the sidewalk, stared at the number for 10 seconds and then tapped on the phone number and held the phone to her ear.

"Hello. This is Derek." A vibrant voice answered.

"Hi, Derek, my name is Kathleen. I was at a Board of Trade meeting last year when you spoke about the Ring."

"Right. How can I help you?"

CHAPTER 4:

The Retreat

"The strength of the team is each individual member. The strength of each member is the team."
-Phil Jackson

As KATHLEEN PULLED up to the hotel where the company retreat was being held, she remembered the first time she went to one of these weekends. The excitement, the anticipation, but then the let down and frustration after she realized nothing really changed.

She remembered how at one organization, the CEO stood up and gave her 15-minute state of the union address to motivate her team, but as she spoke, the words seemed canned and scripted. Then team members would present their game plans and objectives for the year, and then there would be team-building events that were fun for the moment, but forgettable forever.

As she got out of the car to stretch her legs and take in the scenery, she noticed how warm it was for the first weekend in May. This was definitely the place to start something new. After spending time researching various retreat locations, she settled on a beautiful hotel along the Avon River near Stratford, Ontario—known for its famous theatre and festival. Far enough from the busyness of Toronto, but quiet enough for some peaceful sightseeing and reflection.

She unloaded her car, while going over her mental checklist to ensure she had not forgotten anything. How would the group relate to Derek? Who would **be all in** for this journey of change? And more importantly, who would **not be**?

As she walked into the lobby, there was Jane at check-in. Kathleen chuckled to herself because she had purposely arrived hours early to get her mind right and set things up, and here was Jane, probably ready to do the same thing. For all of the challenges they had recently, Jane, if nothing else, was prompt and punctual, like she had always been and would always be.

She shook her concerns from her mind and focused on thinking positive. This will be great; this will be different.

"Great place you picked here, Kathleen," Saul said from his end of the table. "Nothing like the fresh air of the country."

"Thanks. I know the drive was a little long, but I was hoping you guys would like it out here," Kathleen replied.

Saul held up his glass and said, with a big grin on his face, "A toast to Kathleen. For making me remember my Boy Scout days." Everyone laughed and clinked their glasses together.

The group shared their first dinner together at the hotel's restaurant. Derek had said how vital it was that everyone arrive the night before and spend time together. She remembered how he put it: "The group that eats together stays together."

She thought that it would be challenging, but when he told her to not send the typical Outlook meeting invite and instead invite them personally, in a face-to-face conversation, she was pleasantly surprised that everyone was so receptive.

She could not remember one time when the entire leadership team actually sat down and ate a meal together. Somebody was always away or arriving late or leaving early. But now here they were, all eight of them spending time together.

1. Kathleen Brown (COO)
2. Keon Billings (Head of Legal)
3. Lily De La Cruz (VP, Continuous Improvement)
4. Gerald Chow (VP, Banking Services)
5. Saul Perkins (VP, Sales)
6. Mina Zhang (VP, IT)
7. Jane Akash (VP, Human Resources)
8. Marvin Weathers (CEO)

"So, what is in store for us over these next two days?" Lily asked, as everyone was ordering their after-dinner coffees and teas. "I did the homework you asked us to do, but your agenda was a little sparse."

Kathleen responded, "I am in the same boat as you. I pushed Derek to give me more insight into what the two days were going to involve, but you know what he kept saying to me? The group will create the agenda."

"That is different," Lily replied. "This guy obviously has not met Saul yet because we all know Saul always has an agenda." Kathleen and Mina laughed at her joke.

"I heard that," commented Saul from the other side of the table. "Life is an agenda!"

At the end of the meal, everyone got up to head back to their rooms except for Marvin and Kathleen. Marvin had asked her to stay back to discuss the next couple of days.

"What are your thoughts?" Kathleen asked as the last person left the restaurant.

"You beat me to it. I was just about to ask you that," Marvin said. "Let me see…. Well, one thing is for sure, I loved that everyone was here together."

"I know I was thinking the same thing earlier."

"But, Kathleen, they were *really* here—nobody checking their phone. Nobody just waiting for their time to talk. They were really here. They were present."

"I know. It was like everyone was just being themselves. It was nice to see."

"Well, kudos to you for making this happen. The work you had to put in over the past couple of months to ensure that everyone was available, and that everyone remained committed to be here, was not easy. I already feel like we are moving in the right direction."

"No problem, Marvin. But you know how much I want to make this evolution in the organization happen, so thank you for throwing this challenge my way."

"So are you ready to kick things off tomorrow?" Marvin asked.

"I am ready. I have been looking forward to this day for some time now."

DAY 1

Kathleen entered the room just after 8:00 a.m., surprised to see that everything had been moved. Instead of the three tables, three chairs per table, TBO handouts with sales targets, VIP account plans, participant manuals, and TBO swag all laid out as she had planned, everything looked like it had been pushed to the back corner of the room.

Instead, the room was set up in a way she had never seen before. In the middle of the room were eight chairs positioned in two rows facing each other. Below each chair was a pen; a black, red, and blue marker; and a clipboard with a pad of paper. On the two walls, opposite each other, was flipchart paper, stuck to the wall stretching from corner to corner. And the music, *Jammin'*, by Bob Marley was coming through the ceiling speakers.

With his back to her, taking in the beautiful scenery through the floor to ceiling windows at the back of the room, was Derek.

As he heard her walk in, he turned around and said, "Good morning, Kathleen, welcome to…transformation."

"Morning, Derek. How are you?" Kathleen replied, still a little off guard.

"Fabulous. Just fabulous."

"What happened to the room? Marvin, Lily, and I had everything laid out."

"Oh, yes, sorry about that," Derek replied with a smile. "I had to change things up a little. If we want people to change their thinking, I find it is helpful to change their environment."

Kathleen nodded, but was now trying to figure where to put her stuff.

Just after 8:30 a.m., the rest of the team showed up at the room with laptops, tablets, and notepads. Kathleen enjoyed watching all their reactions, as they, too, noticed the rows of chairs and the flipchart covered walls. She almost burst into laughter watching Saul dance to the reggae as he walked in.

The group slowly sat in the chairs facing each other.

Marvin was the last to walk into the room, while talking on his phone. He, too, stopped in surprise as he saw the team sitting in the two rows facing each other. He finished his phone conversation and walked up to Derek to exchange pleasantries.

It was only after everyone was seated that Derek finally left the window, turned the music down, and addressed the group.

"Good morning, all, and welcome to transformation. I am sure you are all finding this set up a little unusual. But if you go on this journey with me and stay open, you will see how powerful we can all make this experience.

"Before we begin, I want to remind you of the conversation we had a few months ago when we first met about commitment. The success of embedding values into our day-to-day operations and positively impacting our culture is based on one thing: your *commitment*. Your commitment to challenge the way you think. Your commitment to being frank in your conversations. And, most importantly, your commitment to act when it is needed. Does that make sense to all of you?"

As Derek looked around, everyone nodded in agreement. "Great, so let's get started with Marvin, as I know he wanted to say a few words."

Marvin stood up and gave a brief introduction. "Good morning, everyone, and as Derek said, welcome to transformation. First, I want to extend a big thank you to everyone for being here. As we all know, the reason we are here is to improve—oops, sorry—transform our culture. Derek, as you already know, has a lot of experience in this area and will be our guide to ensuring the first steps are the right ones. I would like to ask everyone to have an open mind and ear, take notes, but most importantly let's engage in the conversation. The change we are looking for starts with us."

"I also want to thank Kathleen for finding a great place like this, in Stratford, for our retreat, and for running with this project. Let's get the day started. Derek, the floor is yours."

As Marvin sat down, the executives started to clap. Saul added a whistle.

Derek grabbed a chair and placed it beside Keon, who was at one end of the rows. Some of the group moved their chairs so they could see him better, and when all were settled, Derek looked at everyone, smiled, and said, "What does culture mean to you?"

The room was quiet for a moment, then Kathleen said, "I think culture is about customs and tradition. And at work, that would mean it is how we get our work done."

Derek nodded.

Saul said, "Culture is about habits. Good or bad, it's about habits. Oh, and food. In my culture, it definitely has to do with food."

Gerald and Mina, who were on each side of Saul, laughed.

"I think culture is how we feel about our interactions," shared Keon.

"These are all great," Derek said when the room was silent for a moment. "How we get work done. Habits. Interactions. All are on the right track. Dictionary.com's definition of culture is *the customs, arts, social institutions, and achievements of a particular nation, people, or other social group.*"

Kathleen immediately reached under her chair for her pad of paper to make note of what Derek had just said. And then a few other members of the group did the same.

Derek, noticing this, pressed his presentation clicker and then, without even looking at the screen, recited the words that appeared behind him: "Culture represents the things we see, do, and feel, both tangible and intangible. And those tangible and intangible aspects include the social interactions, knowledge, beliefs, customs, norms, and habits that we find all around us. And by around us that includes our family circles, cities, countries, and the places we work."

He changed the slide again and continued, "Here are some interesting and, dare I say, disturbing statistics to capture the importance of this topic. Only 19 per cent of executives believe their company has the 'right culture'.[v]

Companies with strong cultures saw a 4x increase in revenue growth. [vi] In a study of over 1,400 North American CEOs and CFOs, more than 90 per cent said that culture was important at their firms; over 50 per cent said corporate culture influences productivity, creativity, profitability, firm value, and growth rates; but only 15 per cent said their firm's corporate culture was where it needed to be.[vii]

"But for us to clearly understand culture—our culture at TBO—and then transform it, we need to start with values. Culture is the manifestation of values. What do you really value? What do your team members and customers value?"

"To show you what I mean, let me tell you a story about two fictional airline companies—Jetstream and LuxxAir. Both were strong aviation industry leaders with large market shares and were doing extremely well in terms of revenue. Both companies had similar values as well.

Jetstream's Values	LuxxAir Values
• We serve	• Integrity
• We have fun	• Collaborate
• We go above and beyond	• Excellence in all we do
• We are customer centric	• Respect
	• Communication

"At some point in both companies' histories, they went through a crisis. Jetstream had a fatal accident that led to the death of 35 passengers. LuxxAir had a plane crash that led to the loss of 50 lives.

"When the fatal accident occurred at Jetstream Airlines, the leadership team met and asked themselves an important question, 'How do we live out our values as we tackle this incident?' They even presented the question to their employees and held an emergency town hall meeting to gather ideas.

"Jetstream decided to go above and beyond what was asked of them. They opened an investigation on what caused the crash and also conducted safety and maintenance checks on each of their airplanes. They sent their pilots on mandatory training to ensure they were all prepared to handle all scenarios better in the future."

The story was connecting with the group. Some were making notes while others were leaning in and processing the narrative being shared.

Saul asked, "But isn't that just standard airline protocol?"

"It is," smiled Derek, happy to see that Saul had noticed that this was not where the values were coming to life. "But what is **not** protocol, is what Jetstream did next."

"The organization reached out to the families of the victims, and the CEO ensured that at least two members of the executive team were present at all the funerals to represent the organization. The CEO also made an announcement detailing the compensation plan for the families of each victim from the crash. He reached out to local media, so that he could get airtime to address the problems that led to the crash and discuss their plan to ensure how this would never happen again under his watch.

"Jetstream Airlines' share price had dropped after the crash, but after the series of actions taken, stock prices started to return to where they were before the crash. They survived the crisis."

Derek stopped for a moment to let the first part of the story sink in.

"When LuxxAir's accident occurred, the leadership team came together to have a closed-door meeting to decide on their next move. They had their PR team create a press release to communicate their intentions to the public. They reached out to the victims' families, sorted out compensation, and ultimately did all the right things after a crash. But something was off about their culture."

Derek paused again, and this time, he could see the slight hint of anticipation on the listeners' faces as they waited for the distinguishing difference between both airlines' response.

"A month after the crash, emails started to leak out to the press from employees about internal memos sent by the leadership team. The emails also showed employees, who chose to remain anonymous, chatting with one another expressing frustration about the level of mediocrity and lack of excellence when going through a detailed check of the airplanes. One of the engineers even mentioned that his supervisor always rushed them to do a check just to ensure they could do as many planes as possible each day.

"In the end, LuxxAir's stocks didn't recover from the crash. Many loyal passengers stopped flying with the airline, and large corporate accounts and partners stopped working with them. It was evident that their employees and customers lost confidence in the organization."

Derek paused again and looked around the room.

"Both companies went through a crisis. Both developed a plan to survive. One culture thrived. The other experienced an internal meltdown."

"So, what are your thoughts on the story?"

There was silence in the room.

Gerald went first. "It seemed people at LuxxAir used the opportunity to air their frustrations."

"But we are here to talk about transforming culture. What do these stories have to do with culture and values? It sounds to me like some employees were not committed to the organization," Mina commented.

"You're right, Mina. We are here to talk about culture, but in order to transform your culture, we need to realize how **vital** values are to the overall success of your organization."

"You're right, Derek." Kathleen said. "When I think about LuxxAir, I think of an organization that did all the right things on the surface, but because the values and, I guess, culture were not clear or aligned, it ended up destroying everything. It sounds as if the culture was toxic."

"Toxic? I wouldn't say that. I'd say there was a lot of mediocrity," Saul said, as he thought through the scenario in his mind again.

"Well, the reality is that it is part of the culture," Jane added. "Cutting corners, and fear of management, seemed to be part of the culture. And like Derek said, that really starts with values they uphold."

Derek continued. "You can see how impactful culture can be. The employees couldn't take it anymore and decided to start leaking information to the media. That was their way of crying out. Both organizations took actions, but their values had a huge impact on how they navigated the crisis."

Derek scanned the room and everyone was quiet. He knew the comparison of the two organizations always resonated with the groups he worked with.

"Derek, you are really making us think about how we live our values," shared Kathleen. "And as I was getting ready for our retreat a few weeks ago. I came across a stat that aligns with the fallout at LuxxAir. I believe it was a Columbia University study that linked the likelihood of job turnover at an organization with rich company culture is a mere 13.9 per cent, whereas the probability of job turnover in poor company cultures is 48.4 per cent." [viii]

THE RING

"While you think about the story, I want to introduce you to what we will be focusing on for the next two days. Backed by business research and a deep understanding of human dynamics, the building blocks include four key processes and conversations needed to transform a corporate culture. At the Culture Zone, we call these areas the ring."

"The ring of death," Gerald said comically. A few members of the group chuckled.

Derek walked over to the whiteboard and wrote: The Ring of Opportunity.

"Yes, Gerald, it can be a challenge in some phases of the ring, but maybe we can look at things differently. What if we looked at it as a ring of opportunity?"

Everyone was quiet.

"Before I introduce you to the four phases, where would you begin if you were put in charge of a culture transformation project?"

Lily was the first to put up her hand. "My experience has always shown me to think about your end result and then work backwards. And it was actually a principle in a book I've read."

"Ah, yes," said Derek. He smiled, "When I first began leading and supporting organizations in culture transformation, I also used that perspective. And it does work for small organizations, but with larger, more complex businesses, I realized it would not work, due to all the changes organizations go through."

"I have seen many organizations change their leadership team to bring in new perspectives and get rid of old ways of thinking," said Jane.

"Yes, the classic 'burn and churn.' It is definitely a common practice among corporations, but not necessarily always the right one."

"Hey, Marvin, am I getting fired?" joked Saul. "Because if I am, tell me now." Everyone laughed.

"I was thinking about it," replied Marvin, "but I will see how you perform for the rest of the day." Saul grinned, and gave a pretend worried look to the group.

"Based on the conversations I had with you before coming up here, Derek, I would say we need to start with what is most important to us. Both as a team and as individuals," Kathleen said.

"You are pretty close, Kat, and we will do that, but I have found there is another way. And that is to take time to look at the values you already have. Which ones are celebrated, versus which ones are tolerated, versus which ones just hang on a wall?

"So, with that in mind, here are the four areas in the ring required to drive culture transformation are these areas:

- Identity & Assessment
- Embedding Values - OVM
- Development
- Engagement

"Let's first start with Identity and Assessment—determining what values are in existence and how the show up. Think of your values as the behaviours you want to live by as an organization. You have to get really clear on the behaviours you celebrate and the ones you have tolerated. The behaviours to be celebrated are the ones that you know will move your people and the organization forward. Behaviours tolerated are the ones that you know are happening but have not been dealt with. And you know that at the end of the day, tolerated behaviours are hurting the organization. The currently celebrated and tolerated behaviours are the foundation of your culture."

"You do not have to answer out loud, but do think of the answer to this question. Are there behaviours happening in your department or on the teams you oversee that are being celebrated? Are there behaviours on the teams that are being tolerated? When I say tolerated, I mean by everyone: you, your directors, your managers, the frontline performers?"

The room was quiet as he let the question sink in. Whenever Derek presented this question to any executive team he worked with, it always hit home and made them think about who they were as leaders.

"Think of how Jetstream and LuxxAir approached the incidents with their values. One decided to serve their clients and also go above and beyond during the crisis. Another didn't live up to their values at all. We could say respect for their customer, for their team, integrity, and excellence were not lived out in the second case. They were really nothing more than values on the wall."

Though Kathleen had heard a bit of this during the Board of Trade meeting, it seemed she was finally hearing and understanding Derek for the first time. She grabbed her notepad and continued taking notes.

"The next step in the ring is *embedding the values*. When I think of culture, I think of it as a way of life in an organization. It is the unwritten rules by which a group is governed. Many groups allow their culture to naturally develop, but the organizations with great cultures deliberately create and cultivate theirs. When I ask you, is your culture team-oriented or individual-oriented, you should all have the same answer. If I ask whether your culture is a relaxed one, where everyone calls each other by their first name, or it is a formal one, where peoples' titles are always referred to, then you should all have the same answer again. Your answers will indicate which values are embedded. On purpose or by accident. We'll talk more about this as the day goes on."

Everyone was quiet as they processed what Derek was sharing. Then Mina spoke up. "I have worked in both types of cultures, and I find that changing culture is hard. Maybe you could help us more by telling us which one is best."

Mina's question resonated with a few others as they looked to Derek for his response.

"I know you are not going to like this, Mina, but there is not one perfect type of culture. It evolves and must be taken care of to keep it as close to a level of excellence as possible. I would be doing a disservice if I said the culture must be this or that. It must come from all of you. Starting with your values."

Mina nodded. "I guess it's like families—we love our family perfectly, but we are not always perfect as a family."

"Nicely put, Mina," Jane said as she made notes on her pad of paper.

"The third step is development—specifically leadership and management. As we all know, TBO has some huge goals in the way of mergers and acquisitions over the next few years. Mergers and acquisitions usually have a 20 per cent chance of reaching true success.[ix] I'm not sharing this to scare you, but rather to prepare you for what is coming.

"Some of you may be wondering, why is the failure rate so high? Research points to the human factor as a leading reason. The number one person who can influence the human factor in cultural transformation, living out core values, mergers and acquisition, and other major initiatives are you and your managers.

"Organizational success rises and falls on the strategic use of leadership and management practices. You give the vision and critical objectives that need to be met, and your directors and managers lead the execution. They represent you in front of staff members. They also are the voice of the staff members. We have to ask ourselves: how well are they living out what you want as an organization? You cannot give direction and hope they live it out. You have to be sure they are practising exactly what you want. And you must ensure they are doing it consistently, at all levels."

"Consequently, in order to have the culture you desire, you need to truly believe and align with the desired culture, and you must support all leaders that report to you, to ensure that they, too, believe in your mandate and buy into it. If you set a standard of integrity, but the managers decide to cut corners, you will have a culture that's built around cutting corners."

Derek paused to ensure he still had the audience.

"Lastly, we have engagement—value and employee engagement. Here we will focus our energy on how to improve the engagement of our values through dialogue. Consistent dialogue with employees drives engagement and directly impacts morale, motivation, and innovation. Companies with high employee engagement levels have 3.9 times the earning per share compared to their industry peers or competitors. [x]

If you look at the example I just shared, LuxxAir's low employee morale led to staff members leaking confidential messages to the media. Low morale led to actions that contributed to the demise of the organization.

Through our employee engagement model, we will put together strategies that can help us listen to your people better, improve productivity, reduce staff turnover, address diversity and inclusion, and create an environment where employees are happier and more resilient at work."

VALUING VALUES

The team now looked very engaged and intrigued.

Mina leaned forward and shared her thoughts. "This looks very exciting, but going back to step one, Derek, we already have values at the company, are you saying we are going to change them now?"

"Thanks for bringing that up, Mina. I have found that most of the time, an organization's values are sound. But what is lacking is the commitment to them, or should I say a way of embedding them in everyday operations. We are going to look at TBO values and you will decide if the values need to be refined or left alone."

"Before we look at TBO's values though, let's get clear on value categories. Now this is not a new idea, as other books have touched on it, but at the Culture Zone we have a unique way of presenting them. I will explain each of them, and at the end of this conversation, I would like you to give me your honest, objective opinion of what category each value falls under. The primary categories of values are Wall Values, Hidden Values, Multilevel Values, and Core Values.

"Let's start with Wall Values. These are values that are just on your wall. They are values carefully cultivated by the leadership of an organization and have been shared with staff members a long time ago. But that's where it stops. The organization doesn't live by them or even remember them, except when they are being referred to at random meetings or events. They are simply designs on the wall, or powerfully crafted words embedded into employee handbooks, with no level of importance in the association.

"That sounds like LuxxAir," said Lily. "Excellence was one of their values, but the managers weren't living by that." The rest of the team nodded their heads in agreement.

"Good connection, Lily," Derek said.

"Let's move on to Hidden Values," Derek said. "Hidden Values are values that are hiding in plain sight. Wall Values are easily found if you look for them, but Hidden Values are not so easily found, but they are definitely a part of the company's DNA. For example, before joining TBO, who has experienced a leader who was aggressive and led with a sense of individualism? The company may have claimed teamwork as one of their values, but only recognized aggressive leaders and behaviours with individual rewards. Leaders who take all the credit for projects, or push their opinions on others, are looked at as being bold and driven. Consequently, this results in employees being confused because the values the organization really supports (being aggressive) are hidden. An organization says teamwork is the value, but employees know that in order to be promoted, you have to be aggressive, step on people's toes, and work as an individual."

Derek asked, "What do you think LuxxAir's hidden values were?"

The team took time to think through the question.

"Get the job done, regardless of what it takes," Marvin said.

"Exactly," Derek responded with enthusiasm.

"When we talk about Multi-Level Values, we are talking about an organization that lives by different values at different levels."

"What do you mean by that?" asked Keon.

"Our work has shown that different levels in an organization connect with different values. I have seen many situations in which leadership teams speak about a certain set of values as being the values of the company. However, when I speak with managers or team supervisors, the level of values being lived out are totally different. And the ones that frontline staff focuses on are a completely different set of values than those of their managers or executive team."

Keon shared his thoughts. "You are saying that in one company, the leadership could value and promote integrity, strong people leadership, and passion. The mid-level managers could value something else like 'always covering your butt,' 'dominate your people to keep your department in order' and 'passion.'"

Derek nodded his head in agreement. "Exactly, Keon."

"The front line could really value job security and not passion. Or telling half-truths just so they can make it through the day with a horrible manager," Derek added.

The executives in the room shook their heads in disbelief.

"You might not believe me, but it happens. It might even be happening at TBO right now. Some of you are actually living by a value of excellence and performance. While managers below you may be operating by a different set of values—like 'push your people hard.' Which nicely they interpret as performance."

"Like you said, Derek, this is also why the mid-managers need to be developed to support and push the culture we want," Jane said. "If not, we could come up with a great plan here, but could completely fail because of a lack of clarity on what is really important."

"It is sad that the team at LuxxAir was not aware of what was going on until it was picked up by the media," Marvin replied.

"Well, we're not really sure about this. They might have been aware and just ignored it," Saul shared. "Damn hypocrites!"

"What I am asking all of you to consider is that there may be nothing wrong with your values. The real question you need to ask yourself is 'are the TBO values ones that you all can commit to and create a standard that you can hold people to?'"

The room was quiet now as Derek could see that the team was starting to think if they were enabling different levels of values to exist at TBO.

Derek continued. "If you look at the news in recent times, you will find examples of Hidden Values or Multilevel Values directly impacting companies' bottom line. You are probably aware of a ride-share company whose values are 'We are Customer Obsessed' and incidents where this value wasn't upheld by employees, thus costing them millions of dollars through lawsuits, poor publicity, and public trust."

"Wait, what company is that?" Saul asked, with a confused look on his face.

Rather than answer the question, Derek smiled and continued. "And in the financial industry, an investment services company had integrity as a value, yet millions of dollars were intentionally siphoned from their customers' accounts for over eight years."

"So, Derek, what you are saying is that when companies are not living their values, the behaviours that show up can cost them money?" Marvin asked.

"The reality is that many organizations see values as a cool part of forming an organization. It was either a flavour of the month or just something they were supposed to have," Derek replied. "But when it comes to culture transformation and taking your organization to new heights, this is not just an activity. This must be a key pillar on which your entire culture is built."

"When I worked at my previous company, that's exactly what happened," Gerald said. "We got to the office one day and received an email of our new values as an organization and a short video from the CEO talking about why we should all live them. They were placed on the walls by the elevators, in some meeting rooms, on our company laptop screen savers, but that was the last I really heard of it."

"I remember when I first joined a company out of university, part of the onboarding was learning about the organizational values," said Lily. "I was in the cafeteria later that week, and I overheard someone mocking the values, saying this will all die out in a few months. And that was exactly what happened. My managers never talked about them again. Except maybe at performance review time. It seems like this happens often, Derek."

"If you want to change the culture of this organization, you must start at the core. At values. And embed them into your daily operations," Derek said. "Core Values focus on the exact behaviours you want. You identify by them. You live by them. You hire and fire by them. You promote by them. You build your culture from them."

"So what exactly are we looking to do with our values?" Marvin asked.

"First, review them to clarify if these are the core values that you all connect with. Are these the exact values you want? Second, you are going to commit to them as a leadership team. You will live by these values, make decision based on these values and, ultimately, grow by these values. Next, you create a plan or a roadmap to weave these values into the organization's DNA. Everyone at the company must live by these core values and desired behaviours."

CHAPTER 5:

Questions

"Do the best you can until you know better. Then when you know better, do better."

— Maya Angelou

"**I** AM GOING TO ask you a hard question and I want you to think carefully about your response because that will determine how fast or slow this process of culture change and value alignment will take."

Derek took a moment to make eye contact with all eight leaders in the room. "How are you doing as an organization with your values? Do you think all of you—as a leadership team—are living the TBO values in a way that drives consistent results? Before you answer this question, here is a statistic you should be aware of. A Globoforce workforce report found that 54 per cent of respondents who didn't know their company's core values reported being engaged at work, while 88 per cent of those that did know their core values reported high engagement." [xi]

There was silence in the room. And then one of them spoke up.

"I can start." The room turned and faced Marvin.

"Personally, I'd say I am not doing well with our values. Until the board started to highlight culture as a concern, as we looked at acquiring some smaller organizations, I did not consciously think about our company values. I knew they were there as a guiding light, but after your example of LuxxAir and our discussions so far, I think I could do a lot better."

"Thanks for sharing your thoughts and being candid," Derek said.

Gerald spoke next. "Me too. If you asked what our values were before this retreat, I probably could have only listed two of them. I don't think about them. I am so busy running my part of the business."

"Interesting. Who else feels like Gerald?" Derek looked at the group. Saul, Mina, Lily, and Kathleen put their hands.

"Good. I love your honesty."

Derek continued. "For culture to change, we need to start at the top. No question about it. Knowing your values, talking about them, promoting them, and living by them. We are talking about a full embodiment."

Everyone nodded in agreement. "Let's take a closer look at your TBO values." Derek put the values of TBO Bank on the screen.

• Exceptional service	• Passion
• Wealth for all	• People
• Integrity	• Teamwork

"Grab your clipboard and write the answers to these questions:

a. Are these the values we want as an organization? Which should stay? Which should change? Why?

b. Which value will help TBO increase profits?

c. Which values will keep your organization united?

d. Which values support your organization in being grounded, truthful, and legal?

e. Which values will keep you connected to serving your customers and stakeholders?"

The group slowly started making notes.

After a few minutes, Derek continued. "I want you to keep your answers to yourself, as we will come back to them in a moment. One thing I will be reiterating during our time together is if *your values are the fundamental beliefs of your organization, they will lead to the behaviours you want in your organization.* If we want people to live by a certain standard, we must live by that standard, share those standards with them, and evaluate ourselves and them by those very standards."

Derek could see that some were reflecting on what he was saying. Others were nodding in agreement.

Jane spoke up. "I like integrity. It's great to keep truthful and transparent. But I am wondering how we can show integrity? Or even quantify it?"

"I like passion," said Saul. "For us to grow, we need salespeople who are passionate and focused on results."

"But what about too much passion, Saul?" Gerald jumped in. "We've all seen situations in the past where salespeople have been so passionate about their work, they exaggerated sales products or features, and another team has to make up for the miscommunication."

"I hope you are not talking about my sales team," Saul said, with a bit of defensiveness in his voice.

Before Gerald could respond, Derek said, "As we continue to talk and share, I want you to think about your values—personal and TBO's."

"On the wall behind you are your TBO values. I am going to ask you to work in pairs and then as a bigger group, to determine which values we need to keep, and which ones can go. The key distinction you must make is that there must be a clear set of behaviours that can be demonstrated at all levels of the organization, in order for that value to be real."

The group paired themselves, grabbed post-it notes, and then walked over to the wall with the organization's values at the top of the flipcharts. At first there was silence as the groups walked to each of the values. But soon subtle comments turned into conversations, some pairs turning into foursomes while others became separated from the group and stood back, deep in thought.

Soon the post-it notes were going up on the wall under the corresponding values.

After about an hour of discussion, Saul looked at Derek and said, "That was hard, but we did it. We are probably one of the smartest groups you have ever worked with. So, what is next?"

"Great work, everyone," Derek said, smiling in Saul's direction. "And you are right and wrong, Saul. You are a smart group. But that was the easy part. The hard part is that we must all commit to living these behaviours all the time. You are familiar with the phrase, 'what gets measured gets managed?' Well, in the culture transformation business, we say '**what is lived, is leveraged.**'"

Derek paused for a moment for the phrase to sink in. "Meaning, when it is demonstrated on a regular basis across the organizations, it can act as a catapult to overcome challenges and maximize opportunities."

"Oh, I like that!" said Jane, as a few others grabbed their notepads to write down what Derek had just said. "What gets lived, gets leveraged."

"I noticed that you crossed out People as your value. I'm curious to know who did this, and is everyone else okay with it?"

"That was Kathleen, Mina, and me," said Marvin. "Mina said that valuing 'people' sounded nice, but as she thought about what you said about behaviours, it was redundant. We value people by living the other values—service, integrity, passion, etc.

"At first, I was taken aback, but I stayed open, and when Kathleen said she had the same thought from the first day she joined TBO, I realized that Mina was right. It sounds good, but how do I, as you said, demonstrate the behaviour of people."

"I was surprised when I saw her cross it out as well," said Lily, "but as I listened to Mina and Kathleen sharing their thoughts, I also agreed that any behaviour for people would actually fall under 'teamwork.'"

Derek walked over to the wall of post-it notes and started pulling down some of the listed behaviours. "I just removed all of the others that I have seen from past experience that are objectives, not behaviours,'" Derek said, as he walked back to the front of the room. The team looked up at the wall and the values that now remained: Exceptional Service, Passion, Teamwork, Wealth for All.

WORK

"Now that we have agreed on values, let's talk about embedding your values into your organization's DNA. I'm going to tell you a story, and there are two questions I want you to think of while listening." Derek pointed to the screen and read, "A. What stands out about this story, and B. If you were the leader of this organization, how do see you values playing a role in all of this?

Derek grabbed a chair, brought it over to the group and began.

"Quincy had recently joined a manufacturing company as Head of Marketing. A few months after joining the organization, Quincy arrived home one day, withdrawn and quiet. His wife had noticed this and once they had cleaned up the kitchen after dinner, his wife decided to find out what was going on.

"What's wrong, you look a bit down today?"

"Yea…" shared Quincy. "I got some news today that has caught me off guard. One of my directors is not well liked by his team and a few other directors he has to work with. I was under the impression that he was all business, but from the feedback that I have gathered, he is seen as rude, hard-nosed, and inflexible. I have talked directly to his three supervisors to get their thoughts, and they all feel the same way. The challenge is that the guy gets results."

"Really, why won't they complain?" his wife asked.

"They feel the company won't listen. Besides, they are all afraid of negative attacks from him. A number of employees intentionally try to avoid him when he arrives at work. I don't understand how someone like that has risen to that level."

A few days later, Quincy and the Director were in a meeting with other leaders from the organization. The Director spoke about the importance of leadership and building a strong culture in the organization. The leaders in the room seemed to agree with everything the Director was saying. Quincy couldn't believe his eyes and his ears.

A week after this meeting, Quincy was in another meeting with the same Director and heard a question that shocked him.

"What are our core values again? Please, I need those printed and placed in the walls of our offices, so my managers know them and live by them," The Director said. "Quincy, can you get on top of that for us, please?"

"Sure thing," Quincy said. But deep down inside, he rolled his eyes, and thought to himself, I thought one of this company's core values was "We respect one another."

Derek looked at the group and then asked, "Thoughts?"

Gerald spoke first. "What catches my attention is the fact that a Director has risen to this level of leadership and behaves this way."

"It seems leadership loves him and are very proud to have him in that position," Saul said.

"I think you're reading into the story a bit too much, Saul. I don't see that anywhere," Lily cut in.

"Yea…you're right…but the part that says they were 'nodding in agreement' says that at least they respect him a lot," said Kathleen.

"What do you think about the relationship between the values of the organization and the behaviour of the Director? Do you see anything there?" Derek asked.

"I wonder what got him to this level," said Keon. "What if he was a great salesperson or he knew how to handle operations in great detail, or he was an amazing communicator. Yes, we all agree he is violating one value, but the reality is, does he have to live out every value?"

"That's a very interesting question. What are your thoughts, everyone? Should every leader in the organization be able to live out all the values?" Derek asked the group.

"I'd say yes. They should." Jane sat up to address this. "If this is important to the organization, and we are saying that values are the foundation of the behaviours we want, then everyone, from leaders down to frontline staff, should be living the values."

"Everyone?" Gerald asked with disbelief in his tone. "I disagree."

"Okay, Gerald, why do you disagree?" Derek asked.

"I don't think he should be excellent at every value. He is a human being who has challenges— just like all of us. I think you should be good or striving to be great at every value."

"So, what I am hearing from you, Gerald, is that every leader must strive to lead by example in all of an organization's values," Derek said, summarizing the conversation thus far. "You don't have to have mastered it, but you should be leading by example in that area."

The eight attendees nodded in agreement. Derek walked up to the white board and wrote down the point.

"Great, what else do we notice from this story?"

"Obviously, he is not too concerned about the values. I am just being a realist when I say this, but values don't bring money to an organization," Saul said in a matter-of-fact tone. "Yes, they are nice to have, but they don't pay our bills, our salaries, or even make us any money at all."

"I think they do," said Kathleen.

"I get it, values are important…but really?" said Saul. "Do we need to remember *every* value?"

"Great question, Saul," Derek commented. "But before I respond to your question, let me share a story about a pharmaceutical company and a decision they had to make at a crucial moment in their company history.

In 1976, Johnson & Johnson put out a statement of their values and called it a credo. It was solid and clear—and was made readily visible at all Johnson & Johnson offices, even carved into granite wall at the New Brunswick, New Jersey, head office.

The credo was created by the founder, Robert Wood Johnson, and to kick off his role as CEO, James E. Burke was curious if the leadership team and the employees believed in living out the philosophy of the credo. So he gathered the global leadership team together to have a day-long meeting to hear their thoughts on the almost 100-year-old value statement. After much discussion and debate, the team agreed that credo worked and that they all would recommit to displaying the behaviours consistent with it. It may not surprise you that during Burke's time as CEO (1976– 1989), he was credited for the growth of Johnson & Johnson to its current size and prominence.

Those very values that the leadership team and the company built their day-to-day actions on played a huge role in what happened in Chicago 1982.

In September 1982, six individuals died from taking Extra Strength Tylenol that had been tampered with and laced with cyanide. When the news hit the airways, panic ensued. As soon as the deaths were reported, Burke and his team flew to Washington D.C. to meet with the government officials to discuss the next steps. Both the FBI and the FDA strongly encouraged

CHAPTER 5 | QUESTIONS

Burke to limit a recall to Chicago, since a national recall would needlessly frighten the public and possibly encourage copycats.

Ignoring FBI and FDA advice, Burke ordered the recall of 31 million Tylenol bottles (every Tylenol product) from their retailers nationwide—at a cost of almost $330 million (in 2021 US dollars). Johnson & Johnson's was widely praised by public relations experts and the media for its quick response, and when asked why he made the choice to go nationwide in the recall, Burke immediately replied with company's credo: **We believe our first responsibility is to doctors, nurses, and patients; to mothers and fathers and all others who use our products and services.** *J&J's market share in the analgesic market had initially plunged from 37 to 7 per cent during the crisis. Within a year, it rose back to 30 per cent. Within two months of the start of the tragedy, the stock price had recovered back to a 52-week high.*

After a moment, Derek asked, "So what can you gain from this story? What do you see?"

"I find it interesting that the company decided to make a decision based on their values. They lost a lot of money from the onset…but at the end of the day, the decision turned things around for them quickly." Marvin shared.

"My conclusion is that core values should determine the priorities of your company. Those values can shape your behaviours and determine your actions," Jane said.

Derek asked, "So if the core values of the company determine the company's priorities and actions that each staff member should take, how can you, as a leader in the company and the leader of the people, not know it?"

The room fell silent.

"Well, you got us there." Saul replied.

"You are right, Derek," Marvin said. "I want to take full responsibility for this. We do have values, but I've never really talked about them in public, and I don't ask myself if I am living by them. This is something that I need to change. What does everyone else think?"

"I am with you, Marvin," said Mina. "But I will be honest, this will be hard."

"Can we all commit to knowing the values and challenging each other to live by them?" Marvin looked around the room. Everyone nodded in agreement. It seemed no one wanted to say anything.

Derek continued. "To help you make this a little easier, Mina, there are three key points to remember. He walked over to his laptop, pressed a few keys, and then walked over to the TV as the following words appeared:

1. Simplify. Keep your values to a minimum. Easier to remember, thus easier to live.

2. Clarify. One word can mean different things to different people. Your values should not just be identified by one word or phrase. The expected behaviour(s) should be clearly spelled out.

3. Identify. Find values that you connect with and answer these critical questions:

    a. Which value will help your organization increase profits?

    b. Which values will keep your organization united?

    c. Which values support your organization in being grounded, truthful, and legal?

    d. Which values will keep you connected to serving your customers and stakeholders?

4. Verify. Are these the values we want as an organization? Which should stay? Which should change? Why?

"Can you please explain what you mean in number two?" Kathleen asked, looking for further clarification.

"Definitely," Derek said. "And to illustrate my point, let's play a game first. The game will help you answer your question. I will mention a word and you all have 30 seconds to write down exactly what that word means to you. Write down as many words as you can think of in 30 seconds.

"Okay, so the word is fun, write down what the word *fun* means. Remember, you can only use a few words to describe this. Try to limit your answers to words and not sentences. So, use short phrases like The Park, The Gym."

"Terrible example, Derek. I'll never associate fun with the gym, oh NO." Saul was at it again.

"Okay, sorry, terrible example. Hope you all get the point."

The team nodded and spent the next 30 seconds writing down as many words as they could think of.

"Okay, time is up. Marvin, when you think of fun, what comes to your mind?"

"Well, here's what I have: Skating, Skiing, sledding, night out with the guys, working in my shed, that's all I can think of."

"Wow, Marvin, nothing about Lauren at all?" Saul said, teasing.

"Oh crap. Yes, time with Lauren."

Marvin quickly wrote down his wife's name as he turned red in the face.

"Don't worry, I won't tell her, boss." Saul leaned over and patted his boss' back.

Derek looked over to Mina and asked her the same question "So, what do you have?"

"I wrote down: Vacation to Italy, hikes, walks in the park with the husband every evening, craft time with the kids, and cooking dinner."

"Cooking is fun for you?" Lily said with raised eyebrows and a smile on her face. Mina smiled and nodded her head.

"Thanks for sharing, Mina. Isn't it interesting that I asked two people to share what the word fun means to them, and they both have two completely different lists?"

Jane felt the list was not that different, but she decided to keep it to herself. She didn't want to start getting too technical.

"Imagine when a company says **passion** is their value. One word could mean so many different things to 3,000 people. To some it could mean staying early and leaving late. To another, it could mean having fun at the office. While to others, it could mean being obsessive about perfecting a process. To another, it could mean having a ping pong table at the office."

"If you don't spell out exactly what you mean...in other words, what behaviour, or behaviours you are looking for, then you could have over 3,000 interpretations of a value, that could lead to different behaviours. What number two means is that when you mention a value, be sure to be specify the behaviours you are looking for. That way, your value is not open to different interpretations by different people."

Derek looked at his watch. "I know we have to break for lunch soon, so I have two questions I'd like everyone to think about. We will discuss them when you get back.

Based on all your values as an organization,

1. Which one(s) do you believe you are currently very strong at and currently setting an example of?

2. Which one(s) do you believe is a weak area for you?"

ACTION

After lunch, the team came back into the room and noticed that now the room was set up with the tables end to end and their chairs spaced out on each side. As they all grabbed a chair, Derek stood at one end of the table and said, with a smile on his face, "Now we work."

Derek then reminded them of the question he had asked right before lunch. The team discussed their value strengths and weaknesses. Marvin felt that Integrity and Wealth for All were strong areas for him. He felt his behaviour on a regular basis promoted these values. He wanted to work on Exceptional Service and Teamwork.

Kathleen felt Passion and Teamwork were all strong points for her. She felt Wealth for All and Exceptional Service were areas she wanted to work on.

"I actually think you are very passionate about Wealth for All," Lily said to Kathleen. "You talk about it on a regular basis and you make sure the things we do at the office are linked up to this value. I really appreciate that about you."

The rest of the team also shared their areas of strength and weakness. At the end of the conversation, Derek challenged each leader to write a personal commitment to develop their strengths and weaknesses after today's session.

"Every staff member is closely watching your every move and action—intentionally and unintentionally. They will not do what you say, they will follow what you do and don't do."

It seemed the entire team sighed at the same time. It was obvious this was an area they all felt they needed to work on.

The team spent an hour reviewing their values as an organization and decided to use the four key questions to help guide their decision. They agreed to be clearer with the behaviours they wanted for their company values. They also changed the Wealth for All to Prosperity.

The TBO Leadership team settled on their Core Values:

- Prosperity: We exist to create prosperity for all stakeholders—customers, employees, community.

- Exceptional Service: At TBO, we put our customers first. Always create a wow experience.

- Passion: We put our heart and soul into our work. We work with Passion.

- Teamwork: One can conquer a thousand. Two can conquer Ten Thousand. Do your work to make the teamwork.

"I have a great acronym. PEPT!" Jane said with great enthusiasm.

"Well, how about TEPP," Saul chimed in with his big smile.

"I prefer the TEDoubleP Framework," shared Keon.

"Ooo, that's a nice one," Kathleen said.

It seemed the group really liked Keon's suggestion, except Saul.

"That sounds like something a lawyer would say," Saul said, pretending to pout.

"Whatever you all decide is fine," Derek said. "Why don't you take some time tonight to think about it? It's not necessary, but a good acronym would make it easier for your staff members to remember your values."

CHAPTER 6:

The Embedding

"Some people want it to happen, some wish it would happen, others make it happen."
- Michael Jordan

"IF WE WANT to ensure every staff member will be living by the company's core values, then we must find a way to embed the values into your company's DNA, or way of doing business." Derek paused and looked around the room at everyone. "We have to create a set of systems that will ensure all staff members eat, live, and breathe your core values."

ORGANIZATIONAL STRATEGY	IMMERSIVE LEARNING	DISCIPLINED PROCESSES
Key Steps:	**Key Steps:**	**Key Steps:**
Leadership Storytelling	Learning & Development	Hiring & Onboarding
Value Ambassadors	Reviews, Retreats, Redirection	Coaching & Mentoring
Community Engagement	Team Synergy	Performance Management
Visual Campaigns	Driving Innovation	One on One

"You are all now ready for the ***operationalizing values model.***" Derek turned on his laptop and TV monitor to reveal a chart. The title was "The OVM." The chart illustrated the key dimensions.

"To make values live at the core of everything that we do, we need to embed them into our operations. Specifically in the following areas:

    a.   Organizational Strategy

    b.   Immersive Learning

    c.   Disciplined Processes

Derek went on to explain each area. "When it comes to Organizational Strategy, sharing your values with your employees isn't enough. Your values need to be communicated strategically throughout the organization. You need to find a way to consciously and subconsciously promote and remind each staff member of the values."

Katherine put up her hand up to ask a question. "Derek, what have you seen other organizations do to embed values *strategically*?"

"One group I worked with—that was also looking at expanding their customer base by purchasing other companies—first looked at the targeted company's values and how the leaders and employees lived those values. This was done well before looking at any financial numbers. It was hard at first, but through their commitment, the leadership team made the traditional bottom line become the core values of the company. Consequently, their conversations at every level changed to that focus."

"So that really was an example of *what gets learned gets leveraged*," Lily said.

"Exactly, Lily. Great connection," Derek replied.

"Moving on to Embedding in Immersive Learning, your values are not just marketed to your staff," Derek explained. "They all need to be trained on exactly what this is. They need to know that this is very important and that the company is willing to share it with each staff member. In this phase, we will be focused on development through trainings, retreats, reviews, and Team Synergy. Any questions?"

People shook their heads; they were following.

Derek continued. "Lastly, embedding in Disciplined Process. Your core values need to be integrated into every employee-related process. That way, no one can get past the system without having encountered your values. Some areas we will talk about are hiring and onboarding, coaching, and mentoring, performance management systems, and one-on-one meetings."

Derek spent the next few hours discussing each of the phases of the model and the different parts that make up the model, giving examples and statistics of organizations locally and internationally that excelled in the areas. After each of the dimensions, the team would break into groups and tackle one of the pillars of the OVM and then present ideas, challenges, and concerns to the bigger group.

OVM Insights For TBO

OVM AREAS	OVM ACTION STEPS
Leadership Storytelling	<ul><li>Find success stories within the organization (or outside) that can help connect the dots for everyone.</li><li>Strategic sequencing of appealing to emotions then facts.</li><li>Stories are remembered better than facts.</li><li>Storytelling must be creative in design and delivery.</li></ul>
Values Ambassador	<ul><li>Values ambassadors are team members who **embody** and promote defined values.</li><li>Find staff members who are currently living out their core values as a starting point.</li><li>Providing employees with formal, values-based recognition programs reported feeling much more appreciated and are more innovative compared to employees who do not have those programs.</li></ul>
Community Engagement	<ul><li>Involve all staff members to have conversation and dialogue with the senior leadership.</li><li>Inform members so they are engaged through questioning, challenging ideas, and giving feedback.</li><li>Town hall meetings to be held in virtual, in-person, and blended approaches</li><li>Facilitate conversation: instead of leaders informing; they focus on asking questions and listening.</li></ul>
Visual Campaigns	<ul><li>Use visual ways of reinforcing the organization's commitment to core values.</li><li>Creativity is key, so new ways of using visual campaigns can be fresh.</li><li>Like marketing campaigns, the focus is simple: consistent promotion of values.</li></ul>
Learning and Development	<ul><li>L& D is a critical opportunity to teach and develop new skills/concepts employees need for success.</li><li>Consider using proven and possible frameworks to continuously educate staff about their core values.</li><li>Strategically find or create situations to expose employees to different scenarios.</li><li>Debrief on where and how to use values in the solution.</li></ul>
Retreats & Redirection	<ul><li>Retreats are important places to stop, assess, and spend time reflecting.</li><li>Leaders must make time in regular strategic retreats and focus part of the agenda conversation on culture - key questions to ask in the retreat are: - What is working/not working in our culture? - How are we doing as a leadership living up to the values? When have I been living up to the values? When have I not been? - What are some areas we need to get better with our culture?</li></ul>

	- What are the concerns or constraints you are hearing from our people? What side conversations do we need to address?
Team Synergy	• As a team it is imperative to constantly remind yourself of the core values during team meetings, and development. • Constant reference to your values helps to keep it at the top of your mind.
Driving Innovation	• A return on investment by embedding values in immersive learning is innovation. • By ensuring the other aspects are carried out effectively (development, reviews, and synergy), the process will naturally allow for more confident approaches to growth, adaptation, and change. • Driving innovation will happen by creating innovation pods, communicating lessons learned, and celebrating breakthroughs.
Hiring & Onboarding	• Hiring is one of the most important roles of a people leader, not just by HR. • Values must be a part of the interview and onboarding process.
Coaching & Mentoring	• These two activities play a huge role in bringing the values to life by creating opportunities for conversations around the business and how the values can provide a guiding light for employees to perform by. • To sustain the desired values and culture, coaching and mentorship must happen.
Performance Management	• You cannot improve what you do not measure. Leadership must focus on looking beyond traditional performance evaluations. • Focus should be on how employees are living out your values.
One-on-ones	• One-on-ones give leaders opportunities: - to build trust and inspire - to coach, listen, and challenge • People leaders must take this time seriously.

After long hours of learning new ways of thinking, brainstorming how the strategies would be implemented, and documenting how they would proceed, the team was feeling excited but drained.

As they all stood from the table to stretch, Marvin felt compelled to share his thoughts.

"Before we end today's session, may I say a few words?"

Derek gestured, giving Marvin permission to proceed.

"I must say this has been a very intense session for me. Personally, I'm realizing more and more that my job is not just to ensure we keep our doors open as an organization, but also that I need to make sure our culture is intact." Marvin paused and looked at his team. "These conversations have been a real eye-opener for me on how intentional I need to be to ensure the culture we want is lived. I know we still have a full day left, but I just wanted to share that with everyone."

"You're very right, Marvin," Jane said looking up to the ceiling in a reflective mode. "I know this is not the part where we are supposed to start sharing our reflections, but the truth is I've been deeply inspired by this. It's amazing how many people my team is bringing in, and we are not really specific about ensuring these people live up to the culture we want." She looked at her teammates. "Yes, we hire for attitude and technical competence, but we've never really added the culture piece to the entire equation. I mean, we talk about it, but it was never a focal point. I'm learning that we have to be extremely intentional even with that aspect of the business."

"For me, this has been a great session," Gerald added. "My team and I have focused so much of our energy on valuations, financial statements, due diligence, that we've not even thought of value or cultural integration."

"Thanks for sharing," Derek said. "I'm really excited about the opportunities that we're creating as a team. This is the beginning of a great journey. Keep reflecting, keep sharing, keep challenging. There's a lot we can all learn from some of the discoveries you are going through. Just remember your values are the fundamental beliefs of your organization, they will lead to the behaviours you want in your organization. You all should be very proud of the conversations you are having that will allow you to live the values you need and want."

"It is 6:00 p.m., everyone. It's been a day full of learning, insight, and opportunity, and I want to thank you for really being here."

"All right, who's up for drinks tonight?" Saul sat up and stretched. All hands went up as the group laughed and walked out of the room.

"Oh, for anyone interested, I have some passes for a Shakespeare play at the theatre this evening!" Kathleen shared as the team walked out of the room.

DAY 2

The early morning in Stratford is a thing of beauty. Kathleen decided to go for a run along the Avon River to view the water and take in the sights. She arrived back at the inn just in time to grab breakfast, shower, and get ready for the day's session. She was the last to walk into the room.

The room was different this morning. No surprise, Derek had music playing in the background. But for the first time in a long time, no one was on their phones or laptops trying to send out a last-minute urgent email. Instead, they were talking with each other. Saul and Jane were standing near the back wall, standing by the TBO values Derek had put up the day before, and having what looked to be a serious discussion about the values. Marvin was seated beside Lily at the worktable and both were listening intently to what Gerald had to share. At the front of the room were Keon and Mina in a serious discussion and drawing different diagrams on the white board.

As Katherine walked up to Derek, she said, "What's going on? Am I late? Everyone seems to be working on something?"

Derek smiled and replied, "Good morning! Doesn't your team always talk like this before meetings?"

Katherine smiled, picking up on Derek's subtle sarcasm. "Yes, the team does talk, but not like this," she said with wonder in her voice. "Look at them. They are really talking and listening to each other. Look at Marvin, he is just listening and we all know how much he loves to talk."

Both laughed out loud and walked towards the worktable, ready to start the day.

Derek turned down the music, faced the group, smiled, and said, "Good morning, everyone."

The team answered in chorus—brimming with positive energy.

"For those of you who checked out the play yesterday—I hope you enjoyed it."

"Thou never tellest us that thy play only runneth in Shakespearean tone," Saul said, with a big smirk on his face. Everyone laughed at his silliness.

"I was always lost when we read *Julius Caesar* back in high school. I never knew that 30 years later, I would be still lost in the theatre," Gerald commented, sending everyone into another round of laughter.

Derek joined them in the laughter once he understood their joke.

"Welcome back, everyone. I would like to start by reviewing what we have accomplished so far."

Derek walked up to the flipcharts attached around the room and read off some of the statements that the team agreed to on the day before.

"Now that we know and are clearer on where we are going, we need to discuss our identity—our cultural identity."

Derek directed the group to the screen and the following words appeared: "Culture strategy is company strategy."

He asked the team what the quote meant to them.

Lily went first. "It seems what I'm hearing is, regardless of what strategy you put in place, the culture will always triumph?"

"Thanks, Lily. What else?"

Gerald spoke next. "Well, if you don't spend time on values, your strategy or business plans may not be successful. Or as successful as possible."

"Thanks, Gerald, and a great way to phrase that. Culture is critical to your success as an organization. In line with what we said yesterday, this means that culture is serious business. If we do not consciously design what we want, it will design itself. And we definitely do not want it to design itself."

"What we will be doing now is working through a challenging process, but a very worthwhile one, to embed your values and implement your cultural identity. We call it the Culture Roadmap."

Derek pressed his presentation remote, and the following appeared on the huge TV screen:

Step 1 – Create a Roadmap Team

Step 2 – Start Cultural Diagnosis

Step 3 – Determine What You Want

Step 4 – Develop and Work Your Road Map

Step 5 – Review, Reflect, Redo

Many of the group members opened their laptops or a notepad and started writing what was on the screen.

STEP 1 - Create a Roadmap Team

Derek gave them a moment to finish their note taking, then said, "Step one probably sounds very straightforward, but it is not to be taken lightly. We have all heard the phrase: *Teamwork makes the dream work,* and the acronym TEAM, *Together Everyone Achieves More.* But a Roadmap Team is the epitome of the human experience—we cannot go it alone. We are social beings who need each other to survive, and in culture creation, we need each other to grow. Think about how different this journey would be if Marvin was not here? It would feel different, right?"

Many nodded their heads, and then Mina said with smile on her face, "Or if Saul was not here?"

"If Saul was not here, we would probably be finished already," Jane said, teasing her colleague.

"Hey," Saul said in a light-hearted defensive tone. "Fine. These are the last words you are going to hear from me for the rest of the day…. I mean for the next 10 minutes."

Derek continued. "What I have seen work, and I recommend you consider this, is to create a Roadmap Team. You know how in professional sports there is a Head Coach, but then, depending on the sport, you have positional coaches? In basketball, you may have a coach just for the guards, and in hockey there is a coach solely focused on the goalie's development. And in American football, there is coach for each sub team.

"If you're serious about developing your culture, step one is create a culture team, strictly focused on managing the culture building process and sustaining it."

"Isn't that really a focus for HR and Jane's team?" Mina asked, looking for clarification.

"Human Resources is focused on handling the people aspect of the business. But if we want to be different, then we need to take different actions. We want to develop a team that is focused on the culture of the organization. And this team should be made of all different people—and at different levels—because they all impact, and are impacted by, the culture. Remember, culture is not a department but a collection of attitudes, behaviours, and habits. The goal of the culture team is to ensure the plans we discussed yesterday, and ones we'll cover today, are further developed, implemented, and sustained."

Leaning forward, Saul asked, "So what have you seen culture teams look like?"

Derek pointed to the TV monitor, and on the screen was the following list:

The Culture Team should:

a. Ensure there is a representative from different departments.

b. Ensure everyone coming on the team is committed to the culture goal.

c. Create a Culture Charter: a document that clearly states the goal, actions, and expected behaviours of the culture team members.

d. Executive Culture Champions: two to three executives leading the culture project and ensuring that key culture metrics are met.

"I am curious why you specifically ask for two or three executives to act as Culture Champions. In the organizations I have worked at, usually one person is in charge of spearheading the change," Mina asked.

"That is true and typical," Derek replied. "But in these times of constant change, and multiple company projects, have you ever noticed what happens when the key person is not around to make a decision or provide input?"

"Yes. Nothing gets done or moves forward," Kathleen said.

"Yes, so having seen that many times in the organizations I have worked with, I always stress the importance of two champions. It ends up keeping things moving," Derek replied.

"Done!" shouted Saul. "Kathleen is our Culture Champion. What next?" The team nodded in agreement in support of Saul's hearty suggestion.

Kathleen laughed and said, "Thanks, Saul, and Derek. Can you put down Saul's name beside mine? Thanks."

The room broke out into laughter at Kathleen's quick response.

"Perfect. Kathleen, Saul, and I will meet and dive deeper into what the Culture Team could look like," said Derek.

"What I need all of you to do is this: thinking about your respective business units, I want you to select two individuals you recommend working with Kathleen and Saul. And as you think this through, consider these questions to help you with your criteria." And he shared the two questions on the screen for the team to reflect on.

1. Why would they want to be part of the Road Map Team?

2. What evidence have you seen to support that reasoning?

Even before Derek was able to say that they should break off into groups, the entire group was already doing it. Derek smiled to himself and thought, well, that was easy.

STEP 2 - *Start Cultural Diagnosis*

"The second step is what I call the Cultural Diagnosis. In this step, you are looking at two primary aspects of behaviour:

- Identifying your current core values.

- Creating your cultural identity.

"Can you explain a bit more what cultural diagnosis means?" Keon asked. The whole team turned to look at him in shock. It was obvious that Keon's sole focus was no longer on mergers and acquisitions. He was interested in what Derek had to share.

"Thanks for asking. You have heard of an organizational audit, right, Keon?"

Keon nodded.

"An organizational audit is done with the focus on improving operations by identifying the strengths and weaknesses of the organization. Our focus in a cultural diagnosis is looking closer at our behaviours specifically connected to the following:

What is the cultural thermometer of the organization indicating?

What are the top concerns in the company right now, at all levels?

What is our current employee engagement score—overall and per business units?

How are we doing in the area of leadership and development?

How do we get silent/frustrated employees to speak up?

What are our numbers telling us about diversity and inclusion?

"So, Derek, we are looking beyond results?" Kathleen asked.

"Exactly," Derek replied. "We are focused on what we want to create—your vision."

"As a leadership team, we really need to be clear on our behaviours—*intentional and especially unintentional*—because they are the primary reason for the results we are getting," added Lily.

STEP 3 - Determine what you want

After the break, Derek continued. "Let's talk about the personality of your culture. I am going to show you a list of spectrums and I'd like you to identify where your company currently falls, and where you'd like it to fall.

"Just so you know, with the help of Kathleen and Jane, I did a survey of 200 randomly selected staff members at different levels within your organization. Through their responses, I believe I have a rough idea of what your current cultural identity is. Look at these key areas and let us know where you currently are. Remember, try to have a unanimous decision. You're actively building your company culture."

Derek pointed to the screen and the following diagram appeared with the heading: Culture Thermometer.

Step 4 - Develop and Work Your Road Map

Derek asked the team to identify where they thought they were currently on the spectrum and identify where they wanted to be in one year.

After much debate and discussion about the current TBO Culture Thermometer, the team's first draft of the road map was captured in the following table.

Culture Thermometer

Formal & Order	Corporate Stance	Flexible & Open
Competitive	People Interactions	Collaborative
Top Down & Directive	Leadership Style	Relaxed & Friendly
Risk Averse	Risk Level	Risk Tolerant
Focus on Profits	Profit vs. Purpose	Focus on Purpose

Culture Thermometer Insights For TBO

Spectrums	Current State	Desired State	Required Actions
Corporate Stance	• Rigid in approach and mindset - as per needs of the financial business • Survey agreed with report.	• Compliance focused to support transparency for customers. • Rigid response costs at audit time • Open to staff on making changes	1. Maintain mindset and current state. 2. Leadership team to hold bimonthly lunch and learns to communicate to and hear from employees on areas where TBO can be flexible and needs to be rigid in its cooperate stance.
People Interaction	• Very independent. • Has been the culture in the company for some time. • Can feel this inclination towards independence with seasoned staff more than with the new employees.	• Teamwork valued • Collaborate instead of competing	1. Leadership team agreed to discuss at every town hall meeting. 2. Jane committed to build the importance of collaboration into onboarding program for new staff. 3. Leadership team will need to discuss steps to communicate the value of collaboration with seasoned staff.
Leadership Style	• Direct in our leadership style. • Able to adapt to other styles, but not often	• Lead in a more personal way • More trust, less fear.	1. Lily to review the management training for emerging and high potential leaders. 2. Kathleen to update the TBO Coaching Framework & Documentation Process to include

			embedding values for one-on-one and team coaching conversations. 3. Marvin, Lily and will be responsible for ensuring all people leaders are trained on the new TBO Values Coaching Process and retrained annually.
Risk Level	• The group believed that they were in fact risk takers, but the employee survey indicates that the employees thought they were risk averse.	• Determine with employee input, which areas of the business employees thought they were risk averse.	1. Team agrees to have discussion with directors and mangers about areas where they can be more open to risk. 2. Jane and Keon will create a Discussion Guide and Follow up process to ensure constancy in asking for and acting on employee feedback.
Profit vs. Purpose	• Have been heavily focused on profit, but understand the need for purpose. • Employee survey echoed these sentiments	• Pursue purpose with focus on building team, empowering people • Ensuring we clearly communicate to customers our purpose for them	1. Gerald volunteered to spearhead a project to ensure that TBO's purpose and profit idea was added to the onboarding process for all levels. 2. Saul, Mina and Gerald and to write quarterly communications (Top 10 List, articles, mini blogs, video blogs, etc.) for all teams to ensure they can find the profit and purpose balance consistently.

R & R & R

As the group returned to their seats after the final break, Derek also grabbed a seat to sit amongst them. He looked everyone over, smiled and asked, "How do you feel?"

Kathleen was the first to speak. "I feel energized. In all the years we have worked together, I felt like this was the first time we were all in. Not to say that we have not worked well in the past, but we have always been coming and going, with our minds on the other pressing responsibilities of our roles.

I will be the first to admit that is how I have operated. But these couple of days have felt like we really worked as a team."

"Kathleen, I know exactly what you mean and I felt like this retreat was different. Impactful." Mina faced Derek and said, "Thank you for the guidance." Derek smiled and mouthed a "*you're welcome*" in her direction.

"Kathleen and Mina glad to hear your appreciation, but there is one more step we need to discuss, sustainment strategies." Derek pointed his presentation clicker towards the TV and the following words appeared: **Review, Reflect, Refocus.**

Step 5 – Review, Reflect, Refocus

"I am excited that you all feel these couple of days have been valuable, but I am concerned about momentum." Derek's voice become more measured, "You all know that there will be a lot of emails, status meetings, and follow-up conversations to catch up on the projects and people you oversee, once you get back to the office on Monday. So please keep these words at the top of your mind or all of this great work you have done this weekend may fall to the wayside. Review, Reflect, Refocus."

Keon asked, "You have given us so much this weekend, but isn't our Road Map enough?"

"It is a strong start, but as you know, it's how you finish that is most important. That means intentionally reviewing your progress to your desired culture. I recommend reviewing in two ways: one, on your own and at least once a week for 15 minutes. Review all your thoughts, conversations, and actions as it relates to living your values. And two, as a team at least twice a month—and everyone is to share the same, their thoughts actions and behaviours."

"Are you talking about journaling?" Lily asked.

"Yes. Journaling. Note taking. Whatever you want to call it, but the act of recording your thinking and actions allows you to be clear on the behaviours that are working and not working."

"And the personal and team reviews of our embedding values will allow us to reflect," added Saul smiling.

"Precisely, Saul. The reflecting is a natural next step from the review activities. But I caution you to ensure that you practice reflective listening when sharing as a team. By that I mean, repeating back what you are hearing and probing and questioning where necessary to uncover any misconceptions or important truths." Derek could see that many were nodding their heads and absorbing what he was sharing.

"You want us to listen to each other, even after this retreat," Jane asked with sarcastic wonder in her voice.

"Think that was intended for you, Saul," Keon commented. Everyone laughed as Saul threw his hands up in a why-me gesture.

Derek laughed as well and said, "If anyone is interested in my listening training, see me at the end of the day."

Derek then continued, "Reflecting is about checking in with your plans and aspirations and asking yourself and each other if you're still on track. How do you currently feel about the culture? Have you been able to keep the energies of today still burning inside you six, seven months from now?

"If I am hearing you correctly," Lily added, "We all need to be committed to our road map—not just the Road Map Team?"

"Yes, and great comment. The Road Map Team will ensure that key milestones are met, but they will need all your support to push through when changes arise. Changes in terms of personnel, pressing client situations that even right now you are not aware of, or changes in the industry. The eight of you must be each other's lifeline and to maintain focus and alignment on the plans you have worked hard to create over these past few days."

"This is going to be hard," Gerald said quietly.

"Yes and no, Gerald," Derek replied. "Yes, because culture change is never easy. No, because you have spent the time with me and made the commitment even before this retreat to say that this initiative is important. You have started, now you need to maintain."

And that is why the reflecting process will then let you move forward and *refocus*. By using the insights and perspectives you have gained from reviewing and reflecting, you can now decide and be strategic about which priorities need your attention and what actions you will take. This will give you more clarity around needed course corrections and where you may need to invest time and energy to ensure all elements of embedding values are happening."

"As leaders you all know that if you don't do anything differently, things won't just magically change. So make the decision, re-commit where necessary and create new possibilities, opportunities, and conversations. Remember *what gets learned gets leveraged*."

Day two was an eye-opening experience for everyone. They felt relieved that the conversations and work were over, but there was a sense of excitement wrapped around the new culture plan that had been created by all of them.

"It feels so good to have something to go back with," said Saul. "Now we just have to make sure we can run this effectively."

"Well, that's going to be the key responsibility of the Road Map Team. They will focus on keeping everyone accountable and make sure ideas are not just implemented but also sustained over an agreed period of time," Derek replied.

Derek thanked the group for an opportunity to work with them. It was Saul who stood up first to give a standing ovation, in his own special Saul way, "Bravo! Bravo!"

"Designing the program is crucial, "Derek said. "However, going back to the office, actually selling the idea to your directors, managers, and front-line performers, and living out what you expect is going to be very rewarding."

As the group stood up and started talking about the experience with each other, Derek pressed his presentation clicker one last time and the following words from day one appeared:

"Culture represents the things we see, do, and feel, both tangible and intangible. And those tangible and intangible aspects include the social interactions, knowledge, beliefs, customs, norms, and habits that we find all around us. And that includes our family circles, cities, countries, and the places we work."

CHAPTER 7:

The Change

One bulb at a time. There was no other way to do it. No shortcuts –simply
loving the slow process of planting....
- The Daffodil Principle

THE ELEVATOR DOOR opened on the cafeteria floor. It had been 15 months since Savos Restaurants implemented the culture program at their office. It hasn't been perfect, but Guy and his team were committed to ensuring a transformation of the organization's culture.

At first it came as a necessity, but now it had become the mission of the team. One of the hardest things Guy had to do was to let go of the Director of Sales and Marketing for the Ontario East Region. Trevon was a driven sales executive who had worked his way up the ladder with his charm, wit, and creativity. Guy had always admired him from the minute he joined the organization as a marketing specialist 10 years earlier.

As the executive team went through the culture program, it became very clear that many of their leaders across the company were placed in their current positions due to the results they had previously created, not their ability to lead a team or maintain a certain culture. With the new cultural map created, the entire executive team agreed they couldn't continue that way anymore.

"We now have to balance results with humanity. Sales with purpose," Guy shared at a retreat with his team leaders.

Savos decided to call the transformation *The Alignment Project (TAP)*. It was even branded with the symbol of a phoenix. Many of the leaders at Savos saw and believed in the importance of TAP. A few didn't. Trevon was one of them.

"This won't really last, it's just another flavour of the month," Trevon said. He had once mentioned it to another senior manager during one of their conversations after a team update meeting.

On several occasions, Trevon was asked to have regular culture and behaviour conversations with his team—to support the TAP initiative—and he did not. When asked why his team failed to complete team tasks related to the project, his responses were, "I have too much on my plate," or "my team already knows that stuff" and "I really do not think these activities are that important. We need to be closing deals."

Even after four months of coaching from one of Derek's leadership coaches, Trevon's behaviour did not reach the level that was needed of him. Eventually, Guy and the leadership team had to make the call to let Trevon go. It was a tough and expensive call, but it needed to happen.

A year later, Guy is glad he made that tough decision. Not only had the sales and marketing department kept things going but new leaders had also emerged in the department. As a matter of fact, the culture and engagement of the team had soared.

Guy walked out of the elevator and scanned the cafeteria. If he had tried this 16 months ago, employees would probably have had a panic attack because of the fear of leadership. Today, things were different. Things were better.

Staff members were deep in their conversations. Leaders were connecting better and with greater ease with team members during lunch, and there was a real sense of camaraderie in the room.

Guy scanned the room and found the person he was looking for. He grabbed a premade sandwich, a bottle of water, and headed over to sit next to Ravi, the team member he had connected with over a year ago.

"Is this seat taken?"

"Hi, Guy, how are you? No, please have a seat," she said, with a smile on her face. Guy set his food on the table and sat. It had been a long morning filled with several meetings, so it felt good to finally sit down to eat.

"How are you?"

"Doing great," Ravi answered. "It's been a busy week, but I'm glad I get a break before I get back at it."

After exchanging a few more pleasantries, Guy moved to the point.

"I know we had a conversation more than a year ago about how things were going in your department. As you know, we implemented The Alignment Project. How do you feel things are going now, across the organization?"

"That's a very tough question to answer, Guy."

"You know, that's exactly what you said to me last year."

Riva chuckled. "I will say this. Things have improved. I feel better about my relationship with my manager. There seems to be a better approach to how the managers are leading."

"Seems?" Guy leaned in, looking for clarification.

"Maybe that's the wrong word. It's easy to tell that this is new for some managers, but I also know that they need to be commended for their efforts."

"What have you noticed?" Guy asked.

"Take my boss, for instance, I am really impressed on how he's asking more questions, genuinely interested in how I am doing. He even asked me last week if there was anything he could do to better support me."

Guy had a strong desire to pump his fist and yell for joy, but he knew he had to keep his composure.

"That has impressed me," Ravi shared with a smile. "Thank you for listening to us and going out of your way to do this. You didn't have to, but you did."

Guy's phone alarm went off, reminding him of a 1:30 p.m. conference call in about 15 minutes.

"Actually, Ravi, I did have to. I needed to."

Guy quickly finished his food and stood up to drop off his tray.

"By the way, how are you doing? Sorry, I've not asked you."

'Well, let's just say I am having a dirty diaper day," Guy shared.

"A dirty diaper what?" Ravi asked, totally confused. But then she remembered and immediately burst into laughter. It seemed Guy was not about to let the diaper joke go away, even a year later.

Guy walked towards the elevator and pushed the button. He was really glad he had been able to make change around the office, even if it was one person at a time.

Hearing Ravi's story of her manager's attempt to change his management style gave Guy a sense of assurance that the company was making the right moves.

We've lost some, but we are winning some over, he thought to himself. They aren't where he wanted them to be…but this was a really good start.

ANNOUNCEMENT

Marvin walked into the meeting room five minutes late. "I apologize, everyone. My previous meeting ran longer than expected."

Kathleen had already started the meeting, so Marvin immediately sat down and took out his notes.

It was the Road Map Team's final meeting before executing their next moves. Though this was Kathleen's project, she strongly encouraged Marvin to be there. In her opinion, showing his face in the meeting showed how seriously the organization was taking this.

"How are we looking with the communication plan over the next six months?" she asked.

Don, the brand and communications manager, spoke up. "We have a detailed plan now. I will be meeting with Marvin later today to go over his announcement and the other announcements over the next year. We have mapped out two scenarios and have drafted communication for each of them."

Wanting to make sure all areas were covered, Kathleen asked, "How about the Resistance Management plan? How's that looking?"

"We have brainstormed several scenarios that could come up over the next one to two years and will be inviting the appropriate level managers to bi-monthly or quarterly meetings to discuss roadblocks and share resources where possible. I would be happy to tell you the finer details, if needed."

Marvin put his hand up to signal that he wanted to add something. "Sorry to take us back a bit. Don, I know you have already drafted a speech for me to follow at the company town hall tomorrow, but I'd like to request from the team if I can make the speech a bit more authentic?"

"We knew you were going to say that so we made sure the speech sounded as close to you as possible. When we meet, you can take a look and decide if it works."

Don had worked with Marvin as his executive assistant right out of university before transitioning to the communications department three years later. He believed he had developed an ear for what Marvin would try to say to the people.

"Thanks, Don. Looking forward to reading it!"

Kathleen and the team spent the remainder of the hour-long meeting going through the execution plan and details for the next six months. Strategic documents can be great, but execution plans were more impactful with tasks, deadlines, and clear accountabilities laid out.

"Folks, you've all done an amazing job getting ready for this roll-out across the company. Tomorrow is our big day. I'm really excited for this, but more importantly I want to thank you all again for your commitment and efforts."

Marvin smiled as he walked out of the meeting room. Though he initially didn't see a need to be there, he was happy he had attended. As he stepped onto the elevator to go to the top floor for another meeting, Marvin pulled out his notepad and wrote a note to himself: A leader's presence speaks volumes.

The town hall meeting was held in the company atrium and streamed via video to all branch locations across the company. During the first meeting, the entire culture team agreed that presenting a new direction without getting feedback and suggestions from staff members might fall flat upon arrival.

Prior to the meeting, the culture team worked hard to do their internal research—sending out surveys and gathering qualitative and quantitative feedback to better understand the gap areas the company needed to work on.

"This needs to be a real collaboration between leadership and all staff," Saul had said at one of their early Road Map Team meetings. He repeated it at all meetings since then. Derek's words had stuck with him: "**What gets learned gets leveraged.**"

After the agenda and housekeeping for the town hall were shared, Marvin stepped up to make the announcement. With the executive team looking on, Marvin knew this was it. There was no going back.

"Hi, everyone. I have been your CEO for the past two years and I want to first thank you for giving me an opportunity to serve you. You've made leadership fun and fulfilling. As previously announced a few months ago, we are at a point in the company's journey where we are looking to grow through mergers and acquisitions.

"As we started to go through this process, the leadership team realized there was one key area we had not done very well over the past years, and that was our culture. We knew if we were planning to bring in existing organizations, we had to ensure that the people that were looking to us for guidance—all of you—were being guided in the right direction and in the right way. I know I personally failed in that area. And I am sorry. I am very sorry."

The room was quiet as the words hung in the air. The people in the room, and all of those watching online, seemed to really start to pay attention to what Marvin was saying.

"So as a team, we started to think about what type of culture we would like. We knew what culture we did not want. We didn't want a culture of fear. A culture of harassment. A culture that turned branch managers into emperors and the branches their empire.

"We have messed up in the past and we have hurt many. For that, I'm sorry.

"As you remember, to make this happen, we had to start with all of you. We had to start practising the same skills and ideas that our customers like about us—authentic listening, putting aside bias, being willing to shift perspectives. So many of you were part of our varied and unique focus groups, and team-building conversations and, of course, the surveys. I know that I, for one, never want to see another survey in my life."

Those in the room started laughing and some could be heard yelling, "Me too, Marvin," and "Thank the Lord," which brought a huge smile to Marvin's face.

"Our next step as a leadership team was to discuss and determine where we wanted to go as an organization, regardless of the growth plans. We set up a culture team, called the Road Map Team, led by Kathleen, our COO, and represented by one or two people from several the business units.

"With the team, Kathleen has been focusing her energy on spearheading this cultural transformation. This team is undertaking a number of different initiatives to drive the culture conversation. I know you have just started but thank you to Kathleen and the team."

Led by the executive team, the room broke out into applause.

"As a leadership team, we are fully committed to this focus. We might stumble, but we are committed to getting this right soon. And step one, as I have been told, is to hold myself accountable to all of you. Let's start with me; here is what I commit to:

I commit to leading our cultural transformation by leading by example.

I commit to listening more carefully.

I commit to making the tough decisions when needed to show that this is extremely important to the organization.

And I commit to a monthly video blog from me that goes out to every employee in the organization. The goal of the video blog is to keep you updated on our culture journey and what is happening in the organization. That will range from business initiatives, wins and losses, and, most importantly, the great things all of you are doing.

"Someone once told me that organizations really exist in conversation. They exist in the things we talk about, and they die in the things that we do not. And conversations, what we talk about daily, also play a huge role in the opportunity for change. So, my goal is to make culture something that we all talk about so that things change today.

"I sincerely invite you to join this cultural journey. Connect with each other better, serve each other better, and let's work with each other to build a culture that is supportive, people-focused, and exciting. Please join me and the leadership team as we embark on this cultural transformation. Thank you."

The room erupted in applause.

AVOID

Guy and Kathleen met up for coffee at their new favourite spot, Dinein coffee shop in Toronto. With spring in the air and the flowers finally blooming, it was a chance to get out of the office with a light spring jacket and take a walk.

As Kathleen walked into the coffee shop, the smell of coffee filled the room. It seems to be an embodiment of the Toronto lifestyle, fast-paced and ambitious, yet friendly and cozy.

Guy walked in right after Kathleen had ordered her coffee. As he approached the table and sat down, the first words out of his mouth were, "So tell me, how has the Ring been working for you?"

"It has been great. Marvin is fully on board and that makes things very easy. The leaders are adjusting to the new initiatives they are responsible for, but I believe people are trying to move in a new direction. I can sense the excitement in the Road Map Team when they are giving updates. I'm thinking about asking the team to consider a major culture award sometime in the next two to three years. I think it would be great for their hard work to be recognized in the industry.

As Guy sipped his coffee, he nodded in agreement, "Great job so far, and an award would definitely be the icing on the cake."

"You are just over two years into this journey, Guy. What are some key things that I need to watch out for, to ensure we stay the cultural journey course?"

"Oh, you came prepared with questions. Derek really knows how to plant the seeds."

Kathleen smiled, thinking about the coaching conversations Derek and she had been having since the retreat.

"Well, how about this? Let's talk about three mistakes to watch out for on your Ring journey. Mistakes that I made that you could avoid.

Kathleen took out her notepad to start writing. She was not leaving any information to her memory.

"I would say the first mistake at Savos was trying to move too fast."

"But you transformed things in months," Kathleen replied.

"You're right…but if I had to do it again, I would have taken things slower." Guy continued. "We were able to make changes in nine months, but that took a lot of dogged consistent pushing towards the change. We initially came in looking to change things in a span of weeks. Here is the reality. Everyone's behaviour is based on a certain belief that has been embedded over a period of time. Trying to move too fast will only lead to resistance. Our battle should have been more focused on influencing mindsets as we pushed for transformation. We should have given more people chances at the onset."

"You mean you let a lot of leaders go?"

"Not really, but looking back, we probably could have worked with people and been more patient. We should not expect people to change overnight. It takes time to change.

"The second mistake we made was not spending enough time building trust. Trust is such a major human currency. If you do not have it, pure intentions will be seen as calculated attacks. You must ensure you spend enough time building trust with your people. They need to know that not only is the Ring important but that you are also committed to working with them to get it right. If you do not do this, don't be surprised if you have people who would do everything in their power to sabotage the success of the program."

Kathleen nodded as she made her notes.

"One of our managers started spreading a rumour at her restaurant that the program was just management's way of getting rid of some underperformers. By the time we heard about the rumour, the damage was already done. Our VP of HR had to go to the location and a few neighbouring ones to have listening meetings to give employees chance to voice their concerns. We are still having some issues at that restaurant, even with new employees. You don't want that."

Kathleen nodded her head in agreement. She had seen a few of these scenarios come up at TBO recently.

"The third mistake we made was not building enough credibility."

"What do you mean by that?" Kathleen asked.

"People don't pay attention to what we say, but they do pay attention to our actions. When I walked up to make that first announcement about our cultural change, I heard that one of the managers did not believe anything I said. He mentioned to a few other managers that this experiment, as he called it, is just a flavour of the month."

"That's painful."

"Oh, yeah, get used to it." Guy chuckled, as he sipped his nearly empty cup of coffee. "Watch out for frontline staff, managers, directors at your end right now, who are going through the motions, but do not believe in what we are doing. I call them the Above the Line Managers."

"What do you mean by that?" Kathleen asked.

"They do just enough to keep above the line. Above the noticeable line…but they are inflicting a lot of damage on what we're doing."

"So how do you discover them?"

"The leadership team decided to start spending more time with frontline staff members. We also implemented skip-level meetings—some planned, some random, and lunch time with the executives. It opened access to the senior management like never before. I'm sure you know the power and insights gained when you meet with people in the front line. At first, they won't speak at all, but as you build trust, you start to notice and hear things."

Kathleen nodded her head, agreeing.

"Anyway, back to my story, when I heard what the manager had said, I did not get angry. I knew exactly where he was coming from."

"You did?" Kathleen now looked up and stopped taking notes.

"Yes, when I was a manager at one of our restaurants over 12 years ago, he was a new floor supervisor. I was mean then. Mean in the sense that I only tolerated the best from day one. I had not learned how to give people the opportunity to grow."

"Oh, wow."

"Yes. Imagine a man who worked with me for two years then hears about culture and change for the better from me 10 years later. Naturally, he would think this culture thing is a joke."

"What did you do?"

"Well, I drove to the restaurant to have a conversation with him. I brought up what I heard and spent more time sharing about how I had grown since we worked together 10 years prior. I did not focus on his comment. I focused more on the person that he felt did not have the credibility to share that information."

"Did he believe you?"

"Well, that is not for me to tell. That is for him to decide. The best I can do is show the growth and ask him to join the journey. That is why I mentioned points one and two. We have to build trust and not try to change things overnight. If not, we will hit some major walls."

Kathleen thanked Guy for the three pointers. These were key points she would share with the Road Map Team, so they could work it into their strategy. They spent the next 30 minutes talking about business, family, and day-to-day ups and downs before heading back to their offices.

UPDATE

Marvin rushed into the mini recording studio TBO had created for him to record his monthly video updates for internal communication. It was five minutes to recording time and he was running behind schedule. He had planned to arrive 15 minutes earlier.

He said hello to Chris, a member of the communications team assigned to ensure all the recording sessions went smoothly. The culture team had put together a list of talking points, but Marvin had made a few tweaks in the process. Both understood the goal—to keep building trust, keep selling a great culture, and keep transforming minds.

He took a seat at the booth, read his notes one more time, and gave a clear nod that he was ready to record.

Statistics showed that viewership of the monthly videos had improved by 37 per cent since he started recording them six months after the Ring plan was implemented.

"Good afternoon, everyone, and I hope your Friday and your month has been going very well. This is our sixth Culture Talk video update, and I want to send a big thank you to all of you who have viewed and given us feedback so far. We have checked the numbers. The number of times you've listened has grown significantly, and the number of questions and comments we get has been phenomenal. Thank you for being a part of the change we are seeking, and really engaging us.

"Let's start with some basic numbers. As you know, there has been a health crisis in our nation over the past four weeks that has hit our business hard. Many are currently losing their jobs and are fighting to keep their head above water during these tough times. Things are really challenging and we want to make sure we are sensitive to that.

"One of our key values is Exceptional Service, putting our customers first. We want to live up to that. The leadership team is finalizing a plan to help our customers during these times. But I also want to hear from all of you on what else you think we can do to ease the pain and challenges our customers are facing.

"One idea that has come up is to defer mortgage payments or LOC payments. It will affect us as a company, but we have made a commitment to put our customers first. We have to make sure we find a balance between doing that and running our company. Any ideas you have, we want to hear them. Please email them to Lily, and the Process team will look at them.

"On to recognition. I would like to celebrate some great employees from this week who have been exceptional in living up our values.

- **For Exceptional Service**, I want to say a big thank you to Nichole Statin at our branch in Park Hill. Nicole and the team had a customer who had a health crisis at the branch. Nicole not only performed CPR but was able to get a team member to call 911. She and the team have even been able to visit the customer at the hospital this week. That's putting our customers first and we want to say thank you for living up to our value.

- **For Passion,** we challenge our people to put their heart and soul into their work. That is what we have experienced with Carol Misert from our north Guelph branch. We just asked you about ideas of what we can do to help our customers during this tough time. We received several phone calls and emails from Carol about the crisis with several recommendations. She is truly passionate about the customer experience, and when I heard about her several messages and recommendations, I was floored. Thank you, Carol.

- **For Teamwork,** we are recognizing Dayo Fajobi, the Regional Manager of Outremont, Montreal. Dayo has found an amazing way to keep his branch managers engaged and connected during these tough times. He has gone out of his way to bring different locations their favourite desserts and even had a barbeque at his home for the team. We are not asking anyone else to do this, but I want to commend his hard work on building a great team and culture in the region during these times. And if anyone in Outremont now needs a fitness membership because Dayo is feeding them so much, please do let me know.

- **For Wealth,** we are celebrating our Director of Wealth, Kiana Smithson, and her team. They have been pushing to educate all our customers on how to pivot during these trying times, especially with the fluctuations and unpredictability in the stock market. Many have lost a lot of money in the past few weeks, due to this crisis. Kiana and her team have been working overtime to educate clients on what can and should be done. I am very impressed with how quickly they have pivoted and are still find-ing ways to inform and assist. Customers are reaching out and sending their thank yous because of her actions.

"Thank you all for making TBO what it is today. I want to use this opportunity to remind each of you to keep pushing to live out the values in your own special way. Just ask yourself in the morning 'what can I do to live out one value today' and reflect at the end of the day if you have. During your weekly meetings, challenge each other to select one value to work on for the week and spend time reviewing and reflecting through the week."

"This is our only way of growing and transforming our culture. Reminding, refreshing, reviewing...one day at a time. We all have a part to play in making this a great place to work.

We will keep you updated on how we plan to approach concerns like this, moving forward. Thank you for your time and have a great TBO day ahead!"

"How was that, Chris?" Marvin asked as he stood up and pushed aside the microphone.

"Another great one, Marvin. You are becoming a real natural at this."

"Thanks. I feel like I am walking the talk when I do this. Very reward-ing. And thanks for

making it so easy. See you next month."

"My pleasure. I will edit this and then send you the final draft for sign off by Monday."

Marvin nodded and walked out of the room. It was only 1:00 p.m. and there was a lot to figure out, in the midst of a global health crisis. But this was important. For Marvin, culture was now a crucial part of what the organization was about and the only way to succeed when times are good and when times are challenging.

The Culture Ring©

About the Authors

COREY ATKINSON

Famous for bringing a "fabulous" attitude to everything he does, Corey Atkinson is a highly requested leadership and organizational speaker. Corey works with organizations to craft culture solutions that create innovation and change. A VP of Strategic Learning, Professional Speaker, Master Facilitator, and Certified Coach, he has worked with organizations in all industries across North America. He applies critical leadership practices, emotional intelligence, motivational strategies, and the latest learning technologies to support organizational growth, at all levels. He combines corporate coaching insights with design thinking to develop solutions for Leadership Growth, High Performing Teams, Productivity, Impactful Communication, and Innovation.

With over 20 years of leadership and culture change experience, Corey is passionate about the essentials of business success—*leadership, loyalty, and learning.* Deeply interested in team development since high school, Corey is now a dedicated organizational development and learning strategist who delivers highly memorable and meaningful insights and inspiration that repeatedly exceeds the expectations of the client.

AYO OWODUNNI

Ayo is a management consultant with 10 years of leadership and consulting experience in Canada, United States, Kenya, and Nigeria. He is the Director of Training and Development at Prime Target Consulting and specializes in Culture Transformations, DEI, Leadership Development and Strategic Planning. He currently runs a radio show on CBC Radio focused on helping immigrants maximize their potential in Canada.

Ayo is a NCFE Life Coach and Certified Management Consultant with CMC Canada. He has a Master's in Business, Entrepreneurship, and Technology from the University of Waterloo.

Sources & Bibliography

1. The Impact of Company Culture on Employee Engagement, by Lucy Moore. flashpointleadership.com. 2018

2. *The Speed of Trust*, by Stephen M.R. Covey. Free Press Publishing. 2009

Endnotes:

i   Is Your Workplace Culturally Fit? Robert Walters. 2020

ii   Gallup Inc., 'State of the Global Workplace' Report. 2020.

iii   Robert Half Inc., Definitive Guide to Culture, HR Bamboo Research. 2019.

iv   Corporate Culture Matters A Lot, by Susan Adam. Forbes.com. 2016.

v   Global Human Capital Trends 2016: www.deloitte.com/human-capital/global-human-capital-trends-2016.pdf

vi   Forbes, Benjamin Laker, Culture is a Company's Most Powerful Advantage www.forbes.com/sites/benjaminlaker/2021/04/23/culture-is-a-companys-single-most-powerful-advantage-heres-why/

vii   Up Your Culture, "The Case for Company Culture", www.uyc.thecenterforsalesstrategy.com/blog/company-culture-statistics

viii   Entrepreneur.com, www.entrepreneur.com/article/The-link-between-employee-happiness-and-productivity

ix   Entrepreneur.com, www.entrepreneur.com/article/The-link-between-employee-happiness-and-productivity

x   IOS Journals, www.iosrjournals.org/papers/ICIMS/Volume-1/10.pd

xi   Minipulse.com, www.tinypulse.com/blog/methods-bringingcompany-values-to-life

*All website sources were accessed between January 2021 and December 2021.

Author Insights

Click on the links below or use the QR code to listen to Atkinson's and Owodunni's insights about each chapter.

CHAPTER	INSIGHT LINK	INSIGHT QR CODE
Chapter 1	www.valuescultureperiod.com/chapter1	
Chapter 2	www.valuescultureperiod.com/chapter2	
Chapter 3	www.valuescultureperiod.com/chapter3	
Chapter 4	www.valuescultureperiod.com/chapter4	
Chapter 5	www.valuescultureperiod.com/chapter5	
Chapter 6	www.valuescultureperiod.com/chapter6	
Chapter 7	www.valuescultureperiod.com/chapter7	

Looking for more insights, resources, and articles?
Visit: www.valuescultureperiod.com